DRAGON RISING

AN INSIDE LOOK AT CHINA TODAY

JASPER BECKER

DRAGON RISING

AN INSIDE LOOK AT CHINA TODAY

NATIONAL GEOGRAPHIC

WASHINGTON, D.C.

ALSO BY JASPER BECKER

The Lost Country
Hungry Ghosts
The Chinese
Rogue Regime

To Juliette, who was born in China
as this book was written and will live to see
still greater changes.

CONTENTS

PAGES 2–3
The rift between rich and poor— here captured in Shanghai— has never been greater as China tackles economic development head on.

FACING PAGE
Does a democratic future await Communist China?

DRAGON RISING

龍
之
昇
揚

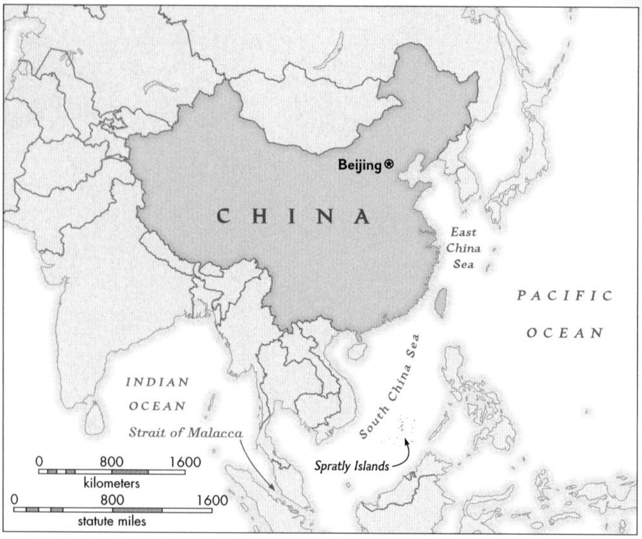

RUSSIA

KAZAKHSTAN

T I A N   S H A N

• Ürümqi

KYRGYZSTAN

XINJIANG UYGU

TAJIKISTAN

TARIM PENDI

AFGHAN.

Taklimakan Shamo

PAKISTAN

K U N L U N   S H A

Boundary
claimed
by India

INDIA

C

Q

Boundary
claimed
by China

XIZANG

(TIBET)

NEPAL

INDIA

BHUTAN

clai
by Chin

INDIA

BANGLADESH

CHINA

Beijing ®

East
China
Sea

PACIFIC
OCEAN

INDIAN
OCEAN

South China Sea

Strait of Malacca

Spratly Islands

| 0 | 800 | 1600 |
kilometers

| 0 | 800 | 1600 |
statute miles

Legend

— International boundary
— Provincial boundary
•••• Disputed boundary
⊛ • • • Selected populated place

Pendi .... Basin
S.A.R. .... Special Administrative Region
Shamo .... Desert
Shan .... Mountain-s

0 100 200 300 400
kilometers
0 100 200 300 400
statute miles

RUSSIA

MANCHURIA
HEILONGJIANG
• Harbin   *Songhua*

MONGOLIA   GOBI

Songhua
• Changchun   JILIN

MONGOLIA   GOBI

NEI   MONGOL   GOL

• Shenyang
LIAONING   • Benxi
Anshan •   • Liaoyang
Liaodong Bandao

NORTH KOREA

GANSU

Beijing
(Peking) ⊛

• Pianguan   HEBEI   • Tianjin   BO HAI
(Tientsin)
Gaoyang •

SOUTH KOREA

• Taiyuan
SHANXI   SHANDONG

YELLOW SEA

JAPAN

NINGXIA HUIZU

Jinghua •   *Fen*   • Panlong

Huang (Yellow)

Huang (Yellow)

C H I N A

SHAANXI   • Xi'an

• Zhengzhou
(Chengchow)   JIANGSU

Bengbu •   Zhenjiang • • Yangzhou
Fengyang •   • Nanjing
HENAN   • Hefei
Huai   ANHUI   • Shanghai
SHANGHAI SHI

EAST CHINA SEA

HUBEI

Songjiang •
Haining •
• Hangzhou   • Ningbo

SICHUAN

CHONGQING
Three
Gorges
Dam

Chang Jiang (Yangtze)

• Wuhan

Yiwu •   • Dongyang
ZHEJIANG

• Chongqing

Dongting Hu

• Wenzhou

Jinsha (Yangtze)

• Liuyang

JIANGXI

HUNAN

• Zhongdian
Yulongxue Shan
+5596 m
• Shigu • Lijiang

GUIZHOU

FUJIAN

Quanzhou •
Xiamen •
(Amoy)

Mekong

• Baoshan
Dian Chi   • Kunming

YUNNAN

GUANGXI
ZHUANGZU

GUANGDONG   • Shantou
(Swatow)

Taiwan Strait

TAIWAN

• Guangzhou   • Dongguan
(Canton)   • Shenzhen
Zhuhai •
Macau •   • Hong Kong
HONG KONG (XIANGGANG), S.A.R.
Zhu (Pearl)

MACAU
(AOMEN),
S.A.R.

Lancang (Mekong)

VIETNAM

LAOS   *Gulf of Tonkin*   HAINAN   SOUTH CHINA SEA   PHILIPPINES

TAIWAN
*The People's Republic of China claims
Taiwan as its 23rd province. Taiwan's
government (Republic of China) maintains
that there are two political entities.*

INTRODUCTION

"**S**o what do you think, are we catching up?" asked the taxi driver who picked me at the Beijing Capital International Airport. It is the question that, if you are a foreigner, especially from a Western country, you get asked everywhere in China.

Usually I answer this query politely by saying something complimentary, but this time I hesitated. After a few months traveling around China to research this book, it was time to come up with a firm opinion.

"What do you mean by catching up?" I countered feebly. "It all depends on what you mean by being modern."

"Well, look at all these new buildings, roads, and cars," he said proudly. "How much longer will it take until we are developed like America or England?"

Beijing's infrastructure has been transformed over the past dozen years. The rundown medieval city has been wiped away and replaced by a forest of plate glass and steel tower blocks. The highways were jammed with shiny new cars and plastered with billboards advertising new computers, mobile phones, and villas.

The driver continued with his line of thinking. "How much do you make? People in China are still poor. We earn so little."

"It is not just about money," I retorted, ducking his question again. I had just returned from Shenyang, a city in Northeast China, notorious for its corruption and where I had interviewed people who had bravely spoken out. "This government can put a man in space, but here on Earth you still cannot say anything against it without being thrown in jail. It is just the same as when I first came to China 20 years ago."

The conversation slackened for a moment as he reflected on this comment. He wasn't offended by the bluntness. My words rang true because, in fact, taxi drivers in Beijing earn very little and were pushing to raise the mileage rate because fuel prices had shot up. If they went on strike, they risked being arrested.

"China is not like the other countries," he said, a little deflated. "We see on the news how people in France or Germany are staging protests. It is going to take time here."

We parted amicably at my front door, but I felt guilty for having been mean-spirited. It was as if I had said that even though the Chinese people had worked very hard, they had failed to pass the exam—Good work but try harder.

Just why discussions (and books) about China, and not Canada, for instance, are framed this way is worth explaining. The Chinese see themselves on a journey to modernize and revive a great and ancient civilization. After a century, the journey is far from over and modernity is spread quite unevenly. The opening chapter of this book presents the road taken after the downfall of the last imperial dynasty. The next chapter visits Shanghai to investigate the enormous effort to transform Chinese cities and create a market economy.

The current modernization phase is bringing change to every part of Chinese society, but there are clear losers and winners. The following chapters describe the workers in the giant socialist factories in the Northeast; the private businessmen getting rich in the Yangtze River Delta; the factory girls working in the export processing factories in the south; and the hard lives of the peasants in central China.

China's emergence as a great manufacturing and export machine and its ravenous consumption of energy and raw materials are examined in the chapter centered on the Yunnan Province, in southwestern China. And the final chapter heads farther south to look at how the rising dragon is affecting small neighbors like Myanmar (formerly Burma) and the world at large.

— JASPER BECKER

BEIJING

WHERE CHINA'S BEEN AND WHERE IT'S HEADED

CHAPTER ONE

Modern China begins with a mystery. In the summer of 1900, the Empress Dowager of Cixi was staying in the Forbidden City and listening to the cannon thunder and crackle of rifles as an army of Boxers, rebel Chinese opposed to foreign influence in their country, attacked the foreigners trapped inside the delegation quarter. Some 900 foreigners from 12 delegations plus 3,000 Chinese converts to Christianity fought off 80,000 Boxers for 55 days until August 14. Once she sent the barbarians some fresh fruit, a token of her benign compassion, but the empress dowager neither ordered her troops who were standing by to save or destroy the foreigners. She simply waited. No one has ever been able to explain why, but the indecision was fatal to the dynasty.

It is easy enough to grasp how close she was to the fighting that over two months cost the lives of 76 foreigners and thousands of Chinese. A walk from the Gate of Heavenly Peace to the British Legation takes less than 15 minutes. The State Security Ministry now occupies the buildings of the British Legation, but above the entrance the lion and unicorn emblem is still there. Over the wall one can still glimpse a handsome bell tower erected in honor of Queen Victoria's Jubilee. Opposite is the large Japanese Legation, now Peking's Communist Party headquarters and the headquarters of the Peking military garrison. The same two large stone lions that marked the French Legation's entrance in 1900 are still there. Nearby are the old French barracks and French school next to the church of St. Michel.

At that time, the world was divided into empires, and the compo-

China's empire technically ended with the abdication of Emperor Puyi, but it still exists today in the form of the People's Republic.

PREVIOUS PAGES
The humiliation of Chinese forces by foreign troops in 1900 led to an obsession with military strength that continues today.

sition of the Legation Quarter reflected this background. The French, British, Austro-Hungarians, Belgians, Dutch, Portuguese, and Russians all had one. The Germans, Italians, and Japanese all wanted one. The Americans were beginning to take over from the declining Spanish Empire in the Caribbean and Latin America and were about to occupy the Philippines.

China, too, was an empire, perhaps the largest in the world. Some 350 million people from dozens of races and many lands owed allegiance to the empress dowager. One of only two women ever to rule the Chinese, she had started life as a pretty Manchu concubine, and yet managed to "rule behind the curtain" with an iron grip for roughly half a century. She literally sat behind a curtain controlling the actions of a succession of emperors she had installed after the death of her husband, Emperor Xianfeng.

When the siege was lifted by an expeditionary force of eight foreign armies that fought their way from Tianjin to rescue their nationals, the 65-year-old empress dowager fled in disguise. After the triumphant foreign armies staged a victory parade inside the Forbidden City, it seemed inevitable that the Qing Empire must collapse and be divided. The Manchu was a foreign dynasty and, as a mark of their subjugation, all male Chinese had to wear their hair in a long braid or queue. The revolution that followed in 1911 was at once a rebellion against the Manchus who had invaded and conquered China in 1644 and an assertion of Chinese nationalism.

It would have seemed inconceivable to any European in 1900 that within a century all the empires would fade into history except for that of the Chinese. China does not call itself an empire, but the People's Republic of China now lays claim to all the territories conquered by the Manchus and rules over the destinies of 1.35 billion people, more even than the British at the height of their imperial glory.

The imperial system of government dates back over 2,000 years to the first Chinese emperor, Qin Shi Huangdi. The king of a small militaristic state near present-day Xian conquered his neighbors and established a highly centralized empire, run on totalitarian lines. When it collapsed not long after his death, the succeeding Han dynasty modified the harsh system of government by adopting Confucianism, a more benevolent philosophy, as the guiding code.

Those who sought to gain lifetime employment in the civil service had to take part in three days of "examination hell" to qualify. The sheds in

which these scholars wrote their essays on Confucianism still existed until the 1920s and lay about a mile west of the Forbidden City, opposite the Chinese Academy of Social Sciences. The most talented scholar-officials were trained at the Imperial Academy, next to the Temple of Confucius in the city's northeast corner. The last examinations were held in 1905, and one can still find in the temple museum the rows of top tablets on which the names of the most successful officials were chiseled century after century.

Like the Ottoman Empire, which ruled over Turkey, the Balkans, and the Middle East, China had come under pressure from the West, whose technological and commercial superiority was becoming obvious in every aspect of life. After Turkey joined the losing side in World War I, the "Young Turks," a group of reformers led by Kemal Atatürk dissolved the empire and forced through an aggressive program of modernization

The Empress Dowager Cixi reigned during the tumultuous period at the turn of the 20th century that saw foreign forces break the power of the empire.

to create a new Turkish nation.

In China, however, the empress dowager, who half jokingly called herself the "Old Buddha," resisted the pressures for change. A poorly educated and vain woman whose closest adviser was the corrupt and gaunt eunuch Li Lianying, she was ill equipped to respond to the challenges posed by the West. The first Western missionaries reached Beijing in the earlier Ming dynasty. The tomb of the great Jesuit Matteo Ricci can be visited in the western part of the city in the middle of what is now a Communist Party training college. The court was always reluctant to allow the foreigners to gain much influence, and a belief in China's innate superiority remained constant until it was reversed in the early 20th century by an equally strong conviction that everything in China was inferior.

At the time the empress dowager joined the Qing court, the Qing Empire was engaged in perhaps the bloodiest civil war in its history, the Taiping Rebellion, brought on by the teachings of such missionaries. It was started in 1850 by Hong Xiuquan, who proclaimed himself the brother of Jesus Christ, and ended 15 years later with the loss of 20 million to 30 million lives. Other uprisings, including those by Muslim minorities in the southwest and other races in Yunnan and Guizhou Provinces to the south, further weakened the empire.

The great Manchu emperor Qianlong, who reigned from 1763 to 1795, had doubled the geographical extent of the empire by seizing territories from the fading Mongol Empire. Between 1741 and 1851, the population rose from 143 million to 432 million. At the peak of his power, Qianlong famously received and rejected the embassy of Britain's Lord Macartney, who reached Beijing in 1793 bringing magnificent gifts and technical marvels like mechanical clocks. Britain was only one of many European powers hoping to break into the Chinese market, but the Qing mandarins kept the traders confined to a small island in Canton, now Guangzhou, at the southern extremity of the empire.

Europe was in the grip of an admiration of all things Chinese, from its sophisticated art to its system of government. European philosophers from Voltaire to Gottfried Leibniz held up China as an example of benign despotism and admired its efficient bureaucracy and religious tolerance. European aristocrats avidly collected porcelains that showed a happy, carefree Chinese people. Beijing was grand by the standards of London or Paris, although by no means the most prosperous city in the empire. London had no more than 100,000 residents in 1700 when Beijing held a million.

Lord Macartney hoped not only to further trade with a treaty but also to establish a permanent embassy at the court in Beijing. This idea proved a great obstacle because the emperor of China, as the son of heaven, regarded no other ruler as his equal on Earth. The British king, George III, could be treated only as the emperor's tributary, but Lord Macartney famously refused to perform the ritual kowtow that would recognize this fact.

The conflict of interests led to the First Opium War (1840–1842) and the Qing Empire's defeat. In the first of what the Chinese call the "Unequal Treaties," the Qing dynasty agreed to open five "treaty ports" to foreign trade and to allow the British to open an embassy in the capital. When the foreign merchants complained that these promises were not being kept, the British and French combined forces to launch the Second Opium War. In 1860, the Anglo-French expeditionary force under the command of Lord Elgin reached Beijing and sacked the Summer Palace. Emperor Xianfeng fled, leaving his imperial concubine Yi—the future Dowager Empress Cixi—to deal with the barbarians. This time, the Qing Empire ceded the island of Hong Kong to the British, and the British and French were at last allowed to open embassies in Beijing. For the first time, a Chinese dynasty had to open a foreign ministry that was not a bringer of tribute.

This event was the origin of the Legation Quarter. The French took over the dilapidated palaces of an impoverished Manchu noble with the title Duke of Qin. The British took the palace of Prince Chun, one of Emperor Kangxi's 36 sons, to whom every Chinese New Year they sent a cart loaded with silver ingots as rent. The Russians already had an embassy and their former legation is now home to the People's Supreme Procuracy.

All this history matters because the defeat of the empire brought on an urge to learn from the West, accompanied by a sense of humiliation, that continues to play a role in China's approach to modernization, trade, and foreign relations. You can still visit the ruins of the Summer Palace by taking a barge on the imperial Jade Canal. Of all the hundreds of buildings scattered over the gardens, the only ones to survive are those built by Jesuit missionaries for Emperor Qianlong. He became a great friend of the painters and architects who built for him the baroque

stone palaces, fountains, and maze.

Over the next 40 years, the empress dowager harbored a distrust and hatred of the Westerners. She had spent her happiest days in the Summer Palace and, although she kept the dynasty in power, she resisted the pressure to modernize.

By comparison, events in Japan took a different course. When the "black ships" of Commodore Matthew Perry arrived off Tokyo Harbor in 1853, the leading Japanese shogun recognized the challenge and embarked on a new course of learning from the West. Japanese society changed from top to bottom, and with the knowledge brought back by thousands of returning students, Japan modernized quickly. The Meiji restoration made the Japanese emperor a symbol of modernization, not an obstacle.

Thirty years later, in 1894, the Japanese navy inflicted a defeat on the Chinese fleet. A year later China ceded Taiwan (then known as Formosa), the Liaodong Peninsula, the Pescadores Islands, and control over Korea when it signed the Treaty of Shimonoseki. From then on, Japan expanded its power, rapidly acquiring its own colonial empire that included Taiwan, Korea, and Manchuria. Japan's military and technological superiority over China tempted it to plunge into the subjugation of China itself, the invasion of Southeast Asia, and World War II.

Spurred by the 1894 naval defeat, a group of young Confucian scholars presented the 24-year-old Emperor Guangxu with a memorandum that outlined an ambitious modernization program. Kang Youwei, perhaps the most famous proponent of reform, was from Canton and in his late 30s when he founded the Association to Protect the Country. Between June and September 1898, Guangxu issued a series of edicts known as the

Hundred Days' Reform, covering education, industry, the military, and political matters and ranging from abolishing the Confucian exams to creating a constitutional monarchy.

By this time, the empress dowager was over 60 and had moved into the New Summer Palace. When one of her trusted generals, Yuan Shikai, informed her of what was going on, she ordered the scholars arrested and executed. She also seized Emperor Guangxu, who would spend the rest of his life as a prisoner on the small island of Yin Tai, on a lake in Zhongnanhai. That lake belongs to a chain of lakes and pleasure gardens that runs through the middle of the Forbidden City. Zhongnanhai is still where the leaders of China live and work. For the last 20 years of his life, Mao Zedong chose to live and work here.

It is not a long walk from Zhongnanhai to reach the houses where the reformers who collaborated on the reform memorandums lived and died. They met at the Yang Memorial Temple, now a museum originally built to commemorate the fate of a scholar-reformer of the Ming dynasty, Yang Jisheng, executed for reprimanding an emperor in a memorandum. In the late 1990s, the original building was a grubby, neglected courtyard house occupied by a rubbish collector. Next door to it was the old Liuyang Guild House, or Huiguan, where Kang Youwei's fellow reformer Tan Sitong had survived on handouts from his fellow countrymen from Liuyang in Hunan Province.

Some scholars escaped arrest, including Kang, but Tan was among the six arrested. On September 28, 1898, their sentence was pronounced from atop the Meridian Gate, the Forbidden City's main entrance. They were taken through Beijing's Chinese quarter, out of the Si Men or "death gate," to a vegetable market, the Caishikou. Their carts were stopped outside the "Broken Bowl" teahouse, where the men gulped down a bowl of rice wine, after which their bowls were broken and thrown away. In front of a crowd, the criminals knelt on the ground amid the rotting cabbage leaves and their sentence was carried out. Afterward, the heads were put in cages and left to rot as a warning to others.

The empress dowager then turned for popular support to a millenarian and antiforeigner sect called the Society of Righteous Boxers. Its members claimed to possess magical powers that made them immune to bullets. The Boxers attacked foreigners, especially missionaries, murdering

Legend has it that the empress dowager diverted funds allocated to the Chinese navy toward building a new summer palace, including this marble boat, depicted in a 1946 photograph, and the result was a crushing defeat at the hands of the imperial Japanese navy.

many of them and forcing others to flee. Then the Boxer army arrived to besiege the Foreign Legations.

The Communist Party still celebrates the Boxer Rebellion as a patriotic movement and presents the ruins at the Old Summer Palace as a symbol of foreign aggression and humiliation. The party also remains determined to avenge the humiliations inflicted by the Japanese and to recover Taiwan, the island lost in 1895. The 1911 revolution that followed is the product of a mixture of impulses: a desire to modernize by importing knowledge and technology from the West while restoring the territories of the Qing Empire and avenging defeats.

The advocates of reform, including Kang Youwei and revolutionary leader Sun Yat-sen, fled abroad, many to Japan, convinced that the Qing dynasty could not be reformed but must be overthrown. A crestfallen and humiliated empress dowager returned to Beijing in 1901 and permitted some reforms to begin, but it was too late. Within three years of her death in 1908, troops mutinied in Wuhan. In 1911, the last emperor of China, Henry Puyi, abdicated. The Republic of China was born and China began a fresh attempt to modernize. Puyi continued to live inside the Forbidden City until 1924, and at least one failed attempt at a restoration was made in 1917. Gen. Yuan Shikai moved into Zhongnanhai after declaring himself emperor, but he died before he could establish a new dynasty.

Dr. Sun found support and backing in the wealthy overseas Chinese communities, and the republican movement became the vehicle for a new Chinese nationalism that stressed the revival of the Han Chinese race. Sun became the first president of the new republic dedicated to reviving the "yellow race" that otherwise, he warned, faced extinction in the global struggle for racial superiority.

European states like Germany and Italy had sought to unify disparate regions on the basis of a shared language and history. The Chinese effort was complicated by the sudden intense desire to reject everything from the Chinese past and to embrace all things Western. Intellectuals like Hu Shi felt that China needed to embrace a complete Westernization. "I unreservedly condemn our Eastern civilization and warmly praise the modern civilization of the West. ... We must admit ... that we are inferior to others not only in technology and political institutions but also in moral values, knowledge, literature, music, fine arts and body physique."[1]

The young rapidly discarded every aspect of Chinese culture, from foot binding to the archaic Chinese in which they hitherto used to write. People copied Western dress and architecture, Western institutions, Western music and literary fashions. Protestant and Catholic missionaries ran many of the colleges and many welfare institutions from hospitals to orphanages. Everything was refashioned—from schools to prisons, from armies to banks to the economy. The May Fourth Movement, which intellectuals led after 1919, called on the Chinese to embrace "Mr. Democracy and Mr. Science."

The Chinese found themselves wrestling with a series of questions that have still not been resolved today: What was the goal of the modernization and what form should it take? How could one forge a modern Western state out of an archaic empire? China was clearly not going to be a constitutional monarchy like Britain, but it did embrace democracy. The building that houses China's first parliament is only a short walk west of Tiananmen Square, but it is kept out of sight in what is now the headquarters of Xinhua, the Communist Party's news agency.

The trouble is that history has no examples of democratic empires. Many parts of the empire began to break away from the new republic, including Mongolia, Xinjiang, Yunnan, Tibet, Vietnam, Manchuria, and Korea. Some became independent states, others fell under the control of warlords or foreign powers. Yet the new generation felt that any loss of territory was a sign of weakness and fresh humiliation. When the Allies awarded Germany's territories in China to Japan under the Treaty of Versailles after World War I, this action prompted 3,000 students in Beijing to march to the Legation Quarter and express outrage.

Shortly afterward, the Chinese Communist Party was founded. Many came to believe that the Russians had found the right model for China. Vladimir Lenin was successfully transforming the backward empire of the tsars into the most modern state of all. Moscow began to wield huge influence in China because Lenin and then Joseph Stalin backed the Nationalist Party (Kuomintang, or KMT) in its drive to unite the country. It helped create a military training academy, the Whampoa College in Canton. After Sun Yat-sen died in 1925 in a house to the north of the Forbidden City, a Whampoa general, Chiang Kai-shek, took charge. He led a well-trained army on a Northern Expedition that by

1927 had taken Shanghai and Beijing and was dealing with the warlords. After the Communists tried and failed to seize power in the big cities, they retreated into the countryside, establishing a number of "soviets" or mini-states in mountainous areas, usually straddling the borders of different provinces. There they stayed for the next 20 years waging a civil war.

The military became the most important institution in modern China. As the Japanese military expansion grew and threatened China's very existence, other voices lost influence. In a state of national emergency, the institutions of a liberal democracy could not put down strong roots. These tumultuous decades cruelly exposed the weakness of the Chinese and provide clues to the fierce militaristic nationalism of Mao Zedong's China.

Chiang Kai-shek depended heavily on American support, while Mao expected Stalin's troops to install him in power. Other Chinese worked for the Japanese as they seized control over most of Asia. Japan's surrender in August 1945 took the Chinese by surprise. Tokyo had a million men under arms in China who were undefeated. Soviet troops moved in from the north, seizing Manchuria and handing over the Japanese weapons to the Communists. The Americans shipped in Nationalist troops and a civil war broke out. Mao promised that if he won, he would introduce real democracy.

Although the Chinese still talk as if a popular revolution took place in 1949, the Communists won power by defeating the KMT forces in conventional military battles. The Red Army, renamed the People's Liberation Army (PLA), became the most powerful agent in the new state, the People's Republic of China. Instead of the liberal democracy envisaged by intellectuals in the 1920s, China became a highly militarized secretive society. The new state soon marched into Xinjiang and Tibet and plunged into a series of major conflicts over the former Qing-dynasty tributary states of Korea and Vietnam.

In many of these conflicts, the United States was China's chief enemy, but its rivalry with the Soviet Union was of equal importance. By 1960, Mao had fallen out with post-Stalin leadership of the Soviet Union, whom he accused of being "revisionists," too ready to abandon the goal of world revolution and a Marxist utopia. As Mao vied for leadership of the global communist movement, relations deteriorated and the two giants entered into a war footing. Beginning in the early 1960s, Mao plunged China into

Chiang Kai-shek (center, with his wife) led China for two decades but ultimately lost power to Mao Zedong's Communists.

a massive, costly effort to prepare for nuclear war and a Soviet invasion.

Beneath Tiananmen Square is an underground highway and metro line that, in the event of nuclear attack, would speed the leadership to command-and-control nuclear-hardened bunkers built in the Western Hills. Since the 1970s, foreign visitors have been taken to a clothing store just to the south of Tiananmen Square, where a trapdoor behind the counter opened up. They would be guided down a long elevator and around a complex of caves that housed schools, factories, dormitories, and even cinemas. This warren is where the population was to survive a nuclear attack and emerge ready to fight.

China had called Moscow its "big brother" after 1950 and modeled all its institutions on those of the Soviet Union. Tiananmen Square itself was designed by Soviet planners as a copy of Red Square, and every year the state would hold vast military parades along the Avenue of Eternal Peace. Mao grew impatient with the Soviet model of central planning that the party followed, however, and plunged the country into a chaotic attempt, dubbed the Great Leap Forward, to reach communism overnight. He abandoned central planning; abolished private property, money, and markets; and even attempted to end family life.

The hysterical rush to create a communist utopia in the "people's communes" foundered on reality. The economy collapsed, and at least 30 million people died of hunger and disease. Mao had set absurd targets to quadruple grain production and to overtake Britain and America in steel production. Local officials inflated harvest figures to fantasy levels and built backyard steel furnaces.

The crisis created a split within the party leadership between the diehard Maoists and the reformers, one of whom was Deng Xiaoping, who introduced sufficient reforms to allow food production to recover. Mao resented being pushed aside and in 1966 launched the Cultural Revolution. He enlisted the Red Guards, middle school students, to "bombard the headquarters" and persecute the "capitalist roaders" like Deng. Millions of party officials suffered assaults and spent years in the countryside or in thought-reform camps.

The endless purges subsided only with Mao's death in 1976. Soon after his embalmed body was put on display in the hastily erected mausoleum on Tiananmen Square, a clique of generals led by Deng Xiaoping staged a coup d'état, arresting Mao's widow, Jiang Qing, and her followers. A new program of change, called "The Four Modernizations," was soon under way. The reformers began experimenting with the first rural markets.

China's new government formally launched the Open Door policy at the third plenum of the 11th Party Congress at the end of 1978, when Deng was installed as the paramount leader. Deng opened the door to foreign investors, established special economic zones, and set about restoring diplomatic relations with the rest of the world.

Few other individuals in history can be said to have done more to change China or the world than Deng. A short, unpretentious, down-to-earth man, he spat in front of visitors, smoked heavily, and cracked jokes. Born in Sichuan to a wealthy peasant family, he had gone abroad to study, ending up in France, where he joined the Communist Party and worked with Zhou Enlai. He rose to eminence in the party as a political commissar in the military and later proved to be such a reliable administrator that Mao turned to him again and again. Despite Deng's being condemned as China's "second capitalist roader," Mao spared his life in the Cultural Revolution. Deng spent years in Jiangxi Province working in a factory, then was brought back to power in the early 1970s as deputy premier, only to be demoted for the second time before Mao's death.

Mao lived and acted as a despotic emperor, but Deng wanted to be different. He did not move into Zhongnanhai and instead lived in an ordinary-looking courtyard house just north of the Forbidden City, opposite a rather grubby-looking public bus stop. He went to great lengths to appear normal: He spent time with his children and grandchildren; he watched football and played cards. When he visited the United States in 1979 as the two countries established diplomatic relations, Deng donned a cowboy hat at a Texas rodeo even though it looked comical and undignified.

Yet Deng was still an autocrat. As he overturned most of Mao's policies, he ruthlessly quashed opposition. He purged the party of the most notorious Maoists and rehabilitated millions of officials, intellectuals, and their families. Deng's ambitions were constricted by the nature of the party apparatus he inherited, top-heavy with poorly educated Maoists. By 1985, he still relied on 15 million party members who were illiterate. The party membership stood at 39 million in 1979 and the 17

million recruited during the Cultural Revolution had to be weeded out. In all, some 30 million party members were judged for their Maoist leanings, rehabilitated, and compensated, a task that took ten years.

The PLA was at once the most powerful instrument at Deng's command and the institution most loyal to Mao. Deng's first task was to halt its massive expansion plans. The PLA's active troop size peaked at 4.75 million in 1981 and Deng shifted a million of them into the People's Armed Police, a new paramilitary force he created to support the regular police. Yet for over a decade, senior PLA officers continued to fill many seats on the politburo and Central Committee. Deng gradually whittled down their numbers by enforcing strict early retirement rules for both officers and party officials. Even for those in senior positions, the retirement age was set at 65.

In reality, it proved harder to destroy their influence. At the top of the party structure is the Standing Committee of the politburo, and their average age in 1982 was 77. Many even older veterans around Deng, like Marshal Nie Rongzhen and Marshal Ye Jianying, were known as the

Immortals. Even those forced into retirement retained their offices, cars, and perks. Many old men held positions in "supervisory committees," or "consultancies," and were popularly known as "mothers-in-law." The grandest of them all was the Central Advisory Commission, and octogenarian veterans continued to attend plenary sessions of the Central Committee and to influence policy decisions and personnel appointments. To implement his policies, Deng appointed two younger men, Hu Yaobang and Zhao Ziyang, described as the Third Generation (Deng himself being a member of the Second Generation).

The reform program that Deng pushed, therefore, depended on approval by men old enough to recall the debates of the 1920s. Deng had to confront basic questions: Was this modernization program just about economic reform? Many veterans wanted to turn the clock back to the 1950s and to restore the Soviet-style system of central planning with its emphasis on heavy industry; others preferred to copy the United States and to create a market economy. Or was it also about political reform? Deng had come to power promising democracy and the rule of law. He had even endorsed the Democracy Wall movement in 1979.

Young activists, including former Red Guards returning from the countryside like Wei Jingsheng, had put up posters demanding real democracy. The majority of the population was under 30 and some of them belonged to the lost generation of "educated youth," exiled to the countryside and now returning to the cities without jobs or an education. They were impatient for radical change and disillusioned with communism; they wanted a Western-style democracy and looked to the United States for inspiration.

Deng freely admitted that he wanted China to learn from the West, to introduce new technology and Western management, and to create a market economy. He thought the Chinese people should become rich. Yet he repeatedly changed his mind about what sort of political system China should have. The party even carried out a few cautious experiments in direct elections before abandoning them. In general, Deng responded to every sign of political unrest with a heavy hand, ordering crackdowns, imprisoning Wei Jingsheng and many others.

The calls for democracy grew louder, led by students and their professors. Student protests spread in late 1986 from campuses in Hefei, Beijing, and Shanghai and spilled onto the streets. Students in Shanghai's

Deng Xiaoping (left, enjoying a Texas rodeo in 1979) was one of China's most reform-minded leaders, yet he ruled with a heavy hand.

Jiaotong University jeered the party secretary of Shanghai, Jiang Zemin, shouting "Who elected you? Was it the people of Shanghai?" When an emergency meeting of the politburo was held in January 1987, the elderly party retirees turned up and threw out the party secretary Hu Yaobang. They suspected he was prepared to give in to the student demands. His replacement, Zhao Ziyang, however, also recognized the need for political reform. Zhao thought that political reform should come from top to bottom and should start within the Communist Party. Zhao proposed separating the party from government, decentralizing state ownership of industry, and making the judiciary and the press more independent.

Far from calming the unrest brewing inside the country, Zhao's program divided the party even further into two factions. When Hu Yaobang died from a heart attack in March 1989, students in Beijing University treated him as a martyr and marched to Tiananmen Square to lay wreaths at the foot of the Monument to the People's Heroes. From then on, the protest movement exploded, spreading to 80 cities across the country and expanding to include workers and peasants. On the anniversary of the May Fourth Movement of 1919, more than a million people in Beijing took to the streets to back the students, who then organized a hunger strike on Tiananmen Square to press their demands. Many officials joined the protests and the police stood by and did nothing. Even after the party declared martial law and tried to move troops into the city, the protest movement swelled and the students erected a statue to the goddess of liberty on the square.

The students demanded an end to corruption, especially among the party members, rather than calling directly for the overthrow of the Communist dictatorship. Such a call would be a counterrevolutionary offense that carried the death penalty. The reforms had enabled the "princelings," the children of senior officials, to exploit their position and grow rich, and Hu Yaobang had lost support among the veterans by arresting and, in some cases, executing the children of top leaders.

The party responded by a campaign against "bourgeois liberalization" and attacked those who called for democracy with nationalist rhetoric. The propaganda harkened back to political debates of the 1920s by saying this movement was tantamount to "all-out Westernization" and that it was foolish to believe that the "the moon is rounder in the West."

Students commemorating the death of Hu Yaobang, the party leader who was dismissed for backing political reform, at the Monument to the People's Heroes on Tiananmen Square in 1989. The prodemocracy protests were crushed by tanks on June 4 that same year.

Behind the rhetoric deployed by both sides, many Chinese who took to the streets in dozens of cities across China must have realized that the chance to end the Communist Party's dictatorship had arrived. Across the communist world, Mikhail Gorbachev was supporting calls for political change. China's gerontocracy, which ordered in the tanks on June 4, 1989, later felt justified by what happened in the Soviet Union. Gorbachev's political reforms led to the downfall of the Soviet Communist Party, the break up of the Soviet Empire, and the independence of Soviet satellites in Eastern Europe.

The on-screen images of unarmed demonstrators being massacred in Tiananmen Square shocked the world, but the party remained unapologetic. The verdict on Tiananmen has not been reversed. Initially, the party concentrated on consolidating its power. It arrested Party Secretary Zhao Ziyang, who had backed the protesters, and staged a witch hunt for his supporters. The PLA strengthened its grip on the party so that the military held nearly a quarter of the seats in the Central Committee after 1989.

The PLA fell under the control of an 83-year-old general, Yang Shangkun, a former henchman of Mao, and his brother and fellow general Yang Baibing. The man chosen to replace Zhao was Jiang Zemin, the party secretary of Shanghai who had been heckled by students in 1986, although the hardline Li Peng wielded most of the civilian power as premier. A Soviet-trained engineer, Li Peng led the country back to central planning, reimposing state control over key sectors of the economy and arresting private entrepreneurs.

China might well have continued down this path had it not been for Deng Xiaoping's second coming. After Tiananmen he had been forced into retirement, blamed for encouraging both Hu Yaobang and Zhao Ziyang, and at first he struggled to get his message across in the domestic media. Jiang Zemin and Li Peng did what they could to stop him, but failed. At the end of 1991, Deng toured southern China, especially his special economic zones of Shenzhen and Zhuhai. He called on the party to deepen the reforms and widen the Open Door policy. By then Deng was already 87 years old; three years later he would fall into a coma, and by 1997 he would be dead.

Deng's Southern Tour, or "Imperial Progression" (*Nanxun*), as it was dubbed, launched a new wave of reforms and a frenzied economic boom. China's first stock market opened in Shenzhen, with mobs of excited investors clamoring to buy shares in the first listed companies. The new wave of reforms transformed the Communist Party's fortunes and may well have saved it.

Many experts, including those in the Central Intelligence Agency, confidently predicted that its end was nigh and that China would break up like the Soviet Union. The student leaders who fled China came close to forming an opposition party funded by overseas Chinese. Many compared the situation to the dying years of the Qing dynasty when Sun Yat-sen and others fled abroad to plot against the empress dowager.

Deng grasped that the party had to respond to the biggest protest movement in Chinese history. This time, Deng won back the confidence of the 40 million overseas Chinese. The billionaire tycoons in Hong Kong withdrew their support for the students and plunged into the new business opportunities that had suddenly opened up. Deng called for more Hong Kongs to be built, and investors poured money into the thousands of special economic zones that opened up everywhere.

China emerged out of the diplomatic freeze imposed after Tiananmen by becoming the darling of the global business community. Western leaders began arriving in Beijing with hundreds of corporate leaders in tow, and each left announcing that a billion dollars in contracts had been signed. In Washington, the U.S. Congress continued to deliberate each year whether to grant China most favored nation trading status, with many still appalled by China's human rights record but with business interests that loomed larger and larger. Yet the situation in China began to be compared ever more favorably to the former Soviet Union.

Chinese officials now claim that the protests were really a demand for more economic reforms, especially among urban residents. In the 1980s, the reforms had started with the countryside, and the peasants had prospered. For the 200 million urban residents, though, including the 100 million working in state factories, there had been no comparable opportunities to get rich. The country's teachers and professors complained bitterly that they earned less than the peasants selling cabbages outside the cramped and dingy apartments they lived in. When economic growth rocketed past 14 percent, urban incomes began to rise.

Beyond the headline statistics, the country remained plagued by unrest. The corruption in the centrally planned industrial economy fueled public anger. The state struggled to pay the salaries of teachers and officials, and there was growing unemployment as tens of millions of state workers lost their jobs. Strikes and protests spread, and when Beijing was forced to rein in the economy after 1995 and call a freeze on the runaway investment, there were fresh doubts about the country's stability.

The Communist Party responded by stoking up a new nationalism that alarmed China's neighbors. China aggressively asserted sovereignty over the distant Spratly Islands in the South China Sea. Then it fired missiles toward Taiwan in 1995 and threatened to invade as that island held its first open presidential elections. Beijing pushed

hard against the pro-democracy movement in Hong Kong when the colony reverted to Chinese sovereignty in 1997.

As Deng Xiaoping and the other Immortals left the stage one by one, the question of how China would reform its political system remained unanswered. Soon after Deng's funeral in 1997, the region was gripped by a political earthquake in the wake of the Asian financial crisis. China censored images of student protests in Jakarta that helped topple the 30-year dictatorship of President Suharto.

China's economy slumped, too, but President Jiang Zemin and his crusty premier Zhu Rongji responded by announcing a huge public-works spending program and a new wave of economic reforms. China privatized public housing and began furiously rebuilding Beijing and other cities. Negotiations over China's membership of the World Trade Organization had dragged on for 15 years, but in 1999 Zhu made a fresh push, traveling to Washington to wrap up the difficult negotiations. The two sides thrashed out a "road map," laying out in detail the future course of economic reforms. China vowed to be a full-fledged market economy by 2014.

The last major Marxist-Leninist dictatorship left in the world stayed in power—but at the cost of embracing capitalism. The Western nations put aside demands that Beijing commit itself to a program of political reform. China crossed into the new century as the only intact great empire, with a fifth of humanity within its borders. Some people, of course, would describe the United States as an imperial power and reckon the European Union to be another superstate. Yet they are nothing like China. Governments elsewhere rest on the consent of the people tested in regular elections and in the courts, but in China the party remains answerable to no one but itself.

China, however, no longer feels like a dark, claustrophobic, and xenophobic land that it was as recently as 1990. A visitor to Beijing finds a city that looks and feels Westernized, as if the goals set out after the 1911 revolution had been reached. The buildings share the same international look as offices and housing anywhere in the world. The shopping malls stock the same global brands by the same multinational companies.

In 1980, the tallest building in Beijing had six floors and housed foreign diplomats. Many Chinese ministries were housed in former palaces that dated back 500 years to the Ming dynasty. The roads were empty of cars, but crowded with bicycles, and half the population dressed in army surplus greens and blues. Everything was rationed and each household stored huge quantities of long "arrow" cabbages to get them through the long winter. At night the streets quickly became deserted, and there was almost nowhere to go for a drink or any entertainment. A few churches and temples had been allowed to open again, but the population was still obliged to attend political meetings several times a week.

It is hard to find more than a few traces of old Beijing. In 1949, it had nearly half a million one-story courtyard houses, but now there are little more than a few hundred. Five brand-new highways ring the city. More than two million people have been moved out of the center that lies inside the city walls to new satellite suburbs. The factories have gone and, in their place, tens of thousands of small businesses have sprung up. This is now a city for the rich to spend their money; the streets are full, day and night, with people shopping or dining and going out to bars and nightclubs. The

The Beijing West railway station, modern but distinctly Chinese.

party meetings have stopped and people now spend their weekends driving out to play golf, ride horses, or fish for trout in the Western Hills.

The Central Business District in the east of the city now has more than 600 skyscrapers that include some of the world's tallest buildings. China has invited famous international architects to design showcase and aggressively modern buildings in the international style. Frenchman Paul Andreu has designed the National Theatre as an egg-shaped dome set in a square lake facing Zhongnanhai. Englishman Sir Norman Foster is building a dazzling airport terminal in time for the 2008 Beijing Olympics. The oval-shaped Olympic Stadium, designed by the Swiss architectural firm Herzog & De Meuron, will sit next to a square national swimming center, the "Water Cube," by PTW of Australia and Ove Arup Engineering. Dutchman Rem Koolhaas is constructing the new headquarters for Chinese Central Television, one of the largest and most innovative office towers ever built.

Beijing has been reconstructed almost as a monument dedicated to modernism by a state dedicated to the spread of science and technology. One bridge in the city even has Albert Einstein's famous formula $E=mc^2$ across the top like a political slogan. It is one reason why some believe that the Chinese state has coped better with the challenges posed by the modern world than has Africa, the Middle East, India, or Turkey. Yet this is forgetting that, for all its real achievements, China still has more poor people than Africa and greater inequality than India.

There are other contradictions. Though China may lead the world in the number of Internet users, the technology is not used to further freedom of expression. The fledgling democracy movement has been crushed at home and abroad and the media remain ruthlessly censored. In brief, China has welcomed "Mr. Science" but not "Mr. Democracy." The country remains ambiguous about other aspects of modernity as well. While it depends on the world for its prosperity, children continue to be taught that historical contact with the West brought humiliation and the Boxers were right to attack the Legations.

While everything in China looks new on the surface, it can seem unchanging underneath. The way China is governed remains largely unreformed, and Beijing's architectural planning reveals an uncertainty about the future. The Communist Party still occupies hundreds of buildings across Beijing that bear no name plate revealing their function but are

The Olympic Stadium rises in Beijing as China looks forward to showcasing its prosperity and new architecture in 2008.

guarded by armed soldiers. The party remains a remote and secretive organization. The nation's rulers continue to live in Zhongnanhai like emperors past, and Mao's portrait hangs over the entrance to the Forbidden City even as China turns its back on his revolution. Despite the plethora of new construction, one thing is missing: a new parliament building. The Communist Party, uncertain whether there will ever be separation between party and state, has omitted to design a new set of office buildings to house the institutions of the central government. Since 1989, China has put aside thinking or talking openly about the recent past or politics. Just when, or how, China will resume that part of its search for modernity is a matter of endless speculation. A snapshot of a China in the midst of an unfinished revolution can merely stir the imagination.

2

SHANGHAI

MODERNIZING THROUGH CAPITALISM

CHAPTER TWO

Shanghai is where modern China took shape and it is still the only city in China that actually feels like a big city. Like New York, London, or Paris, it has real streets lined with trees, magnificent civic buildings, pleasant parks, comfortable suburban houses, and university campuses with lawns and ivy-covered halls.

Reviled in the 1920s and '30s as the "whore of the East" or admired as East Asia's greatest metropolis, China owes its first modern factories, banks, schools, universities, financial markets, newspapers, orchestras, and film stars to Shanghai. From its position at the mouth of the Chang Jiang (Yangtze) Delta, the city spread new technology, new fashions, and ideas to the vast hinterlands beyond.

Then in 1949, after nearly 20 years in rural China, Chairman Mao Zedong's Red Army marched triumphantly into Shanghai. If you walk down the famous Bund, the row of massive buildings that once housed the great banks and trading houses, there is a statue of Marshal Chen Yi, the military commissar who led the peasant army into the city as the defeated Nationalists boarded ships to retreat to Taiwan. In the magnificent entrance hall of the Shanghai Municipal Council hangs a photo taken in May 1949 showing Shanghai's new rulers, dressed in drab tunics, standing on a balcony declaring the establishment of the Shanghai Municipal People's Commune.

Shanghai became a bastion of ultraleftism. Chen Yi and his cadres moved into the headquarters of the Hong Kong & Shanghai Bank, the

Glittering Nanjing Road is China's leading shopping destination, evidence of Shanghai's return to commercial prominence.

PREVIOUS PAGES
Against a backdrop of rapidly developing Pudong, a young couple enjoys a romantic moment along the Bund.

greatest Western financial institution in Shanghai. The factory workers who produced half the country's industrial output became the vanguard of the new proletariat utopia. The factories were nationalized, the markets closed, and the capitalists fled.

One of the Gang of Four who directed the Cultural Revolution was Wang Hongwen, a former textile worker at the No. 17 Cotton Mill in Shanghai. Members of Shanghai's richest family, the Rongs, who owned 30 textile factories by the 1930s, fled abroad or found themselves in labor camps.

The great Shanghai diaspora took their skills and capital to Taiwan, America, and, above all, Hong Kong. That British colony replaced Shanghai as China's greatest port and center for film, publishing, and fashion. Taiwan, which remained under strict martial law until the late 1980s, a temporary military fortress from where the Kuomintang (KMT) planned to reconquer China, never managed to re-create Shanghai's cosmopolitan greatness.

At the start of the 1990s, the city's great revival began. Chinese leader Deng Xiaoping gave the signal and the central government began pouring vast sums into Shanghai. It was in a dismal state, a crumbling, decaying ruin that advertised to the world the failures of Chairman Mao's revolution.

Almost nothing had been invested in Shanghai's infrastructure or housing stock for 40 years. People lived crammed into an average of just 40 square feet per person, the least living space in the country. They worked in factories using machinery that was 50 years out of date. The city was bankrupt. The cost of supporting Shanghai's retired workers and officials ate up the city's entire gross domestic product.

The city was filthy and dirty. The factories bordering Suzhou Creek poured a toxic stream into the Huangpu River, which oozed through the city center and was as noxious as a bath of acid. The cost of cleaning up and dredging the lethal sludge from the bed of Suzhou Creek was calculated at a billion dollars.

The population was literally dying off, and not just from cancer and lung diseases. Shanghai had taken the lead in enforcing the one-child policy in 1979 and the fertility rate had fallen to just 1.6, well below the replacement rate. From 1993 onward, the city had actually

A parade of tanks carries the triumphant Red Army into Shanghai in 1949, ushering in four decades of neglect by Communist officials.

recorded a negative population growth. While in the 1980s some 180,000 children were born each year, the figure had dropped to fewer than 70,000 by 1997. The shortage of children meant that hundreds of primary schools had to close down. Without substantial new immigration, Shanghai was doomed.

Shanghai was not the only great Chinese city to face these problems; all cities suffered from the same neglect. Chairman Mao's enthusiasm for egalitarianism went hand in hand with vehement hatred of cities and urban life. Beginning in the 1960s, he emptied Chinese cities until China had such a low proportion of city dwellers that it was rivaled only by Pol Pot's Cambodia. However, of all the cities of China, Shanghai was perhaps the only one to keep a negative population-growth rate into the 1990s.

Shanghai's crisis deepened with the launch of the 1979 reforms. The central government in Beijing still drew half its tax income from

Shanghai's factories, which supplied 80 percent of the country's textile needs. Deng Xiaoping agreed with his advisers that it was too risky to start experimenting with reforms in Shanghai. Instead, he favored areas near Hong Kong, granting Guangdong Province a raft of special concessions, including tax holidays, and he appealed to the overseas diaspora to come back and invest. As a gesture to win their confidence, Deng appointed Rong Yiren, nephew of business tycoon Rong Zongjing, as president of the China International Trust and Investment Corporation (CITIC), China's first post-1979 merchant bank.

Rong Yiren had stayed behind when the rest of the family scattered around the world in the 1930s, and he disappeared during the Cultural Revolution. He reappeared after Deng ensured that Wang Hongwen and the other members of the Gang of Four were in prison. Deng eventually made Rong Yiren a vice president of China, an honorary post. Rong Yiren's son Larry Yung is now one of China's richest men and owns a vast mansion in the English countryside.

One branch of the Rong family had fled to Hong Kong, where Rong Yuan set up the Da Yuan and Nanyang cotton mills, enterprises that helped lay the foundation for Hong Kong's postwar manufacturing boom. Hong Kong light-industry manufacturing companies, including those set up by the Rong family, began to move production across the border into China in the 1980s and began undermining the profitability of the Shanghai state factories. With antiquated machinery and cradle-to-grave welfare systems, the Shanghai mills could not compete with the new factories employing cheap peasant labor.

To run Shanghai, Deng appointed Jiang Zemin, a cautious former engineer who had studied in the Soviet Union and worked in Romania. Jiang came from a middle-class family in Yangzhou in the Yangtze Delta and as a student in Shanghai during the 1940s had joined the Communist Party. Not far from the Bund, I once walked past a middle school where he had been a teacher after graduating. When he became party secretary, the Shanghainese mocked him for being a useless "flowerpot" because he did nothing to tackle Shanghai's problems in the 1980s.

The city's shortages of electricity and water worsened and in the winter of 1986–87, Shanghai was rocked by student protests. Tens of thousands gathered in the People's Park, the former Shanghai race course, and then marched to the Bund demanding to meet Jiang. When he arrived to confront the students at one of the universities, he was mocked and humiliated by the students calling for democracy and radical change.

Jiang had pondered privatizing the factories or returning them to their original owners, but in the end decided on another solution; he drew up a plan to create a new Shanghai on the other side of the Huangpu River, called Pudong (literally "east of the Pu"), which would be a special economic zone bigger than Shenzhen, bordering Hong Kong. In the meantime, he sat on his hands as the frustration built up in Shanghai and many cities.

When the volcano erupted in Beijing in early 1989, Jiang moved to silence pro-democracy voices, closing down newspapers and preventing the university students from mobilizing the factory workers. In this way, he suppressed the democracy movement in Shanghai without calling in the military. As a reward for his loyalty and political skills, Jiang was promoted and moved to Beijing as the new general secretary of the Communist Party.

The party swung to the left and the plans for Shanghai were kept on the shelf until the end of 1991, when Deng Xiaoping moved to take the initiative. He made a tour of southern China and while visiting special economic zones made a call for more and faster reforms. The new policies were all aimed at reviving urban China and creating new markets for property and finance. A centerpiece of the reforms would now be Shanghai. Deng gave the green light to the Pudong project.

At this crucial turning point in Shanghai's history, Jiang, as usual, did nothing, but he eventually gave his support to Deng's initiatives. Once he had done so, there was nothing halfhearted about the effort and Jiang was well placed to direct the scheme. Bringing many followers with him to Beijing, the leadership became top-heavy with the "Shanghai Gang." The very fact that China was now being run by Shanghainese was a symbol of Shanghai restored to its former eminence.

Under the leadership of Zhu Rongji, Jiang's former deputy, the project started building a replacement for everything on the other side of the river. The developments ranged from the Lujiazui financial center—a new version of the Bund with its grand bank and insurance buildings—to a container port that would be bigger than Hong Kong's. Where else in the world has there been such an effort to revive a great city like Shanghai? And in so short a time? By 1999, the central government alone had spent 30 billion dollars on infrastructure, dwarfing the sums invested in Shenzhen. Shanghai boasted 5,000 cranes working on new roads, expressways, tunnels, sewage systems, a second airport, a metro system, and new housing. By early 2006, something approaching 200 billion dollars had already been spent and construction is still going on at a furious pace.

The city raised nearly 40 billion dollars by selling land leases to private developers, many from Hong Kong and Taiwan who belong to the Shanghai diaspora. The population decline has been reversed by an influx of half a million outsiders, including 200,000 Taiwanese, 100,000 from Hong Kong, and about 50,000 non-Chinese. Many more have come from other parts of China to buy up the new apartment blocks and offices.

In the space of just 15 years, Shanghai built some 8,000 high-rises, including 5,000 in the city itself, all of them taller than any building that had existed before 1980. In Pudong, Japan's Mori company is committed to building the world's tallest building, the 101-story Shanghai World Financial Center. Its nearest rival is in Taipei.

The city says it has attracted some 25,000 overseas-funded enterprises that have brought 46 billion dollars of overseas capital. Many have gone to Pudong with its free-trade zone, high-tech park, export-processing zone, and new port.

Some three million residents have been relocated out of old Shanghai and now live in nine new satellite cities that have been built around the periphery. Thousands of old, dirty factories have been closed down and demolished. In their place, Shanghai has created a huge new steel plant at Baoshan, the largest in modern China, and General Motors has invested in an equally dazzling car plant, creating a new industry for the city.

The most impressive piece of showcase modernism is the German-built Maglev train line that connects the city to its new international airport in Pudong. It cost an estimated 1.2 billion dollars, but the trip is so short that the train only briefly touches the top speed of 269 miles an hour and will probably never recoup its costs.

Towering office and apartment buildings continue to rise around Shanghai, displacing residents at a developer's whim.

By the time the city plays host to the World Expo in 2010, the new city should be completed, a model of a modern major metropolis. Can it be judged a success? It is hard to decide what to make of it all or to find out what the Shanghainese themselves think of it. At first Shanghai tends to strike the visitor as immensely exhilarating. The scale of the energy and money unleashed, the brash self-confidence of the project and its sheer gigantism are all overpowering.

On later visits, it can seem a little depressing. After a while, one feels a sense of exhausted dislocation—the construction sites, the crowded roads that take you to places identical to the one you just left. The dull, repetitive architecture is wearying. Everyone you meet is a stranger, too, and seems as confused as you are. It certainly looks modern. Hollywood has begun to use Shanghai as a backdrop for films set in a sanitized but disturbing future where the characters suffer from a postmodern anomie. "Local leaders think the higher the buildings, the more modern and the more successful they have been," says Professor Ruan Yisong of the Tongji University's School of Architecture and Design. "And the more neon lights, the more dynamic the city has become."

Development is a harsh process with little or no public consultation. Developers have free rein to evict people, and often do so overnight. More than 219 million square feet of old buildings, half of Shanghai's old neighborhoods, have been torn down in the past 15 years. It is hard to think of another country in the world where three million people could be moved out of their homes so quickly. The real estate and construction companies have reaped considerable and easy profits of around 30 percent a year, if only because land has been made so cheap by the ease with which residents could be evicted.

Reports of the corruption and kickbacks and the occasional resistance by residents have been quickly suppressed. One story that became known concerns one of Shanghai's most famous landmarks, the girls' school in the former French concession where the Communist Party of China held its first meeting in 1921. Buildings around it were demolished, their residents forced out by 300 police when they refused to move quickly enough. Part of the land has been turned into a fashionable and expensive shopping and dining area called Xin Tiandi, or New Heaven on Earth, with the highest rents in the city. Shanghai leads all Chinese cities in forced relocations, with more than 850,000 households demolished since 1993.

Yet many of the tower blocks have been left empty years after they were completed—40 percent by 2000. Many are of such poor quality that they will need major repairs after ten years. And the proliferation of high-rises has created a city with a population density of 5,790 people per square mile—far higher than that of New York, Paris, or London. The sheer weight of all these towers (and people) is causing the city to sink into the swampy banks of the Huangpu River. Experts say Shanghai has sunk by about eight feet since 1921 and is now sinking at a rate of roughly half an inch a year. Even the futuristic Maglev is threatened by subsidence.

What has happened to Shanghai has been happening to cities all over China. The buildings and methods are invariably all the same. Yet for me, and probably for many Shanghainese, there is something tragic about the haste in which it is being done. A wonderful architectural heritage is being discarded.

My favorite hotel is the Astor Hotel, which also claims to be the oldest in Shanghai. It has a magnificent classical facade overlooking the Huangpu River, and in its dim corridors hang faded photographs of former guests, including Charlie Chaplin, Ulysses S. Grant, Albert Einstein, and Bertrand Russell. A glass cabinet holds the original land deeds dating from 1857, when the Richard family founded the hotel. A framed painting shows guests in 1882 admiring the very first electric street lamp lit in China. It never took long for a new Western invention to reach Shanghai. The hotel even boasts that it had central heating and hot and cold running water five years before any hotel in America.

Although it was once hailed as Shanghai's most grandiose hostelry and perhaps East Asia's, my vast, wood-paneled bedroom and the marble pillars of the hotel's ballroom promised luxury that it could no longer deliver. Groaning pipes dripped water on my sheets and sputtered forth a stream of brownish water that had a harsh chemical flavor. Downstairs in the "world-famous Richard's Café," surly staff dished up a strange version of Western food.

In its own inimitable way, the Astor Hotel explains why Shanghai's leaders thought they had to remake Shanghai from inside out and from top to bottom. After 50 years under state ownership, it was hard to go back and restore either the plumbing or the mentality of the staff. It was easier to pull everything down and to start again.

When Charlie Chaplin stayed in a suite in the Astor, he would have looked across the steel-girder bridge that spans the Suzhou Creek to the Bund. Ships from all over the world would have been crowding the Huangpu River waiting to unload at the Hong Kou wharfs just around the corner. The dockhands lived in crowded tenements not far away.

These days, international trade is carried out by huge container vessels too large to dock in the river. Shanghai had no choice but to build a new port some 30 miles away on an artificial island where the huge ships could be unloaded by modern cranes. Without this investment, Shanghai could never hope to recapture its status as a great port.

Opposite the Astor's entrance is the Russian Consulate. Back in 1927, when the Chinese Communists prepared to stage an uprising and take over Shanghai, they were assisted by Soviet revolutionaries staying at the consulate. The uprising, supported by dockhands and textile factory workers, did seize power for a while, until KMT troops marched into Shanghai and crushed the first people's government.

At the Astor Hotel you can even sleep in the bedroom (Room 311) where the Communist leader Zhou Enlai and his wife, Deng Yingchao, lived for two months hiding from the purge that the KMT unleashed. Zhou, who had studied in France and retained a taste for croissants all his life, was never one to slum it even in the midst of a bloody rampage.

When they demolish the Astor, as they probably will, all this history and association will be lost. In Communist Party literature, Shanghai was a moral cesspit run by brutal gangsters operating opium dens and prostitution rackets where everything and everyone was for sale, a decadent "city of adventurers" where honest Chinese workers were cruelly exploited by capitalist imperialists and which could only be purified by a violent revolution.

Every child grows up believing this. When one walks around looking at the surviving architecture, it comes as a surprise to realize that it tells a very different story. Walking along Suzhou Creek and across the Szechuan Bridge, I came across a magnificent post office built in 1920; it was being restored and turned into a museum. This building was once the largest post office in China and no expense had been spared in its design and decoration. Outside, the pillars were decorated in green-and-gold wreaths; inside, the counters made from marble seemed absurdly grandiose for the mundane and humble task of selling stamps.

Just around the corner and down a side street, it was astonishing to come across what looked like a Greek temple fronted by a portico held up by four Doric pillars. This building was designed by Chinese architect Guo Yangmo in 1928 for Shanghai's Chinese Banking Association. It was now occupied by a commercial college, a haberdashery, and some other rather unsuccessful businesses. Bored salesmen in short sleeves

A profusion of sampans crowds the Suzhou Creek in front of the Astor Hotel (right, with the Soviet consulate behind) in 1927.

slumped around slurping tea and reading newspapers. Like so much of Shanghai, the building seemed to belong to an earlier and superior civilization that had been abandoned, and now the Shanghainese squatted there in growing squalor.

Nearby was a neglected art deco cinema that was finished in 1928 and, despite being a protected building, appeared about to be demolished. Farther up the street a similar art deco building, designed by architect Ladislaus Hudec and finished in 1931, had once housed the Christian Literature Society.

All the buildings show a civic pride and a commitment to build in Shanghai the very best that the world had to offer. Shanghai was, of course, a city built by immigrants, but these modern elegant buildings were commissioned by owners who weren't about to leave after making a quick profit. They were here to stay. Most were built and finished in the

1920s and 1930s when Shanghai boomed and Europe struggled in the aftermath of World War I.

The former home of the Shanghai Municipal Council, a complex of 400 rooms created in the European New Classical Renaissance style was finished in 1924. It was built to last and now houses the welfare administration for retired soldiers and Communist officials and a medical instruments company.

Just around the corner are three art deco buildings that form a set: the Metropole Hotel, dating from 1934; Hamilton House; and the Commercial Bank. The original owner of the Metropole, a Mr. Saxon who was also chairman of the Jewish Confederation, ensured that every

item from the gilded spiral staircase to the hexagonal-style pendant lamps exuded luxury and sophistication. Until the early 1920s Shanghai had only 1,700 Jews, but some were prominent citizens. They traced their origins back 160 years to when some 700 Sephardic Jews reached Shanghai from Baghdad, Spain, Portugal, and India.

One family, the Sassoons, who arrived in 1844, built the luxurious Cathay Hotel (now the Peace Hotel) and lived in a fantastic nouveau-Tudor villa with a minstrel's gallery and a fireplace big enough to roast an ox. Like so much else from the past, their history and their contributions have been swept under the carpet. The former Shanghai Jewish Club has become the Shanghai Musical Conservatory. Sir Victor Sassoon's home is now the Hotel Cypress.

The Ohel Rachel Synagogue, which Sir Jacob Elias Sassoon built in 1920 in memory of his wife, Rachel, remains closed to the public and has been used by the city's education commission. The majestic building is now on the World Monuments Fund list of the 100 most endangered sites. The Chinese government refuses to let the small Jewish community open or reopen a synagogue, because Judaism is not one of the five official approved religions.

Another great family, the Kadoories, left Shanghai with the legacy of a white, wedding-cake-style mansion that is now the Children's Palace. In Hong Kong the Kadoories still own China Light and Power, Hong Kong's largest power utility.

The vast majority of newcomers who built Shanghai's wealth were Chinese like the Rongs. That family's empire was founded by Rong Zongjing, a product of China's "self-strengthening movement" that Li Hongzhang, a top Qing dynasty official, launched in the 1880s. Rong's first textile mill in Shanghai opened in 1878 and, renamed the Shenxin No. 9 Mill, was closed down only in 1996. The Rongs also built the first modern shipyards in Shanghai and the first Chinese-owned shipping company, the China Merchants Steam Navigation Company, was established here.

As all this building happened, the locus of Chinese commerce shifted from the interior to the coast. Shanghai replaced Pingyao in Shaanxi Province as the financial capital of China. The new Shanghai must, therefore, be judged in many ways. Does its new architecture

Modern Pudong, the new city across the Huangpu River from old Shanghai, was built from scratch after 1991.

match in sophistication and elegance what is being torn down? And more importantly, can the city ever recapture the role that it has lost?

Tokyo is now by far Asia's biggest financial center and is second only to New York. It seems unlikely that Shanghai would ever replace it. It even seems hard to see when, or if, Shanghai will be able to outdo Hong Kong in any respect. The volume of trade passing through Shanghai still lags behind Hong Kong and Singapore, although it will soon match Rotterdam, once the world's largest port.

Shanghai's financial markets are a long way behind Hong Kong's. As one of the favors granted to Shanghai, the central government determined that Shanghai, along with Shenzhen, could host the country's new stock market although there were other cities contending for the honor. In 1990 Shanghai's new trading floor was actually in the old ballroom of the Astor Hotel. It has since moved to a high-rise office tower in the middle of the Lujiazui financial district in Pudong. In 1992 the market went entirely electronic, and traders now

play the market from their desks so the trading floor is deserted. When I tried entering one morning, the doorman stopped me and I noticed that only six people seemed to have turned up for work.

In 2000, when the market peaked, the government boasted that Shanghai's stock market would overtake Tokyo's and become the world's third largest before 2010. The stock market authorities said 70 million people had opened trading accounts. Indeed, everybody in Shanghai seemed to be "stir-frying stocks," and you could find traders spending their day in front of huge screens watching the numbers.

When the stock market bubble burst in 2001, the number of active traders shrank to fewer than 500,000. The value of the listed shares fell to around 145 billion dollars, not much more than Malaysia's exchange in Kuala Lumpur. The weekly trading volume dropped from a high of 178 billion yuan in February 2000 to just 31 billion yuan in February 2005. Most of the 130 securities firms went bust and hundreds of brokers were arrested for corruption and fraud; the government had to create a six-billion-dollar cleanup fund to compensate small investors.

Almost all the companies listed on the Shanghai and Shenzhen stock exchanges are large state-owned enterprises (SOEs) in the process of turning into modern corporations. These enterprises remain firmly in the control of parent companies that are owned and controlled by Communist Party officials. They remain poorly supervised, opaque, and often corrupt organizations. A Ministry of Finance investigation found that 90 percent of them cook their books to inflate performance.

The SOEs had been solely responsible for paying for their workers' pensions, housing, and medical care. In the new system, the enterprises are supposed to pool what pension and welfare funds they have and channel them into a common fund that would be invested in stocks and bonds. In practice, those enterprises with funds have been reluctant to share them with poorer companies or the money has been embezzled. As most state enterprises cannot cover their pension and other obligations, and the state has been reluctant to place its shareholdings into the market, the project failed. The state owns the majority of shares of the biggest enterprises and there are not enough potential investors willing to buy them.

The best-run state companies have chosen to be listed in Hong

The Shanghai Stock Exchange, a rising star on the world financial markets until its 2001 crash, continues to struggle.

Kong or on the New York Stock Exchange, and private companies have been barred from raising capital at all. Most people now prefer to keep their savings in the four big state-run banks. These, however, have lent heavily to the state-owned companies or to real estate and construction companies. The state banks have been slow to adopt commercial lending practices and, with an estimated 30 to 40 percent of their loans believed to be nonperforming, the banking sector is technically insolvent. Untangling this mess could take a long time and Shanghai's long-term future is mortgaged to the project to make the capital markets work. Although it may take decades, Shanghai does have the potential to become a world-class financial center.

The new generation of urban workers is already taking out private pensions and health and life insurance policies. The value of occupational pension funds, for example, is supposed to grow by 80 billion to 100 billion yuan annually, reaching one trillion yuan over the next ten years. Over time the rural population will also be encouraged to take out insurance policies that, given the size of China's population, could create a vast pool of savings bigger than that of any other country. The insurance and pension funds will have to find safe investments, and a large share will have to be put into company shares either at home or abroad.

The recent setbacks have forced China to allow foreign investors to take stakes in banks, insurance companies, and brokerages, partly in order to recapitalize bankrupt financial institutions and bring Chinese operating procedures in line with international standards. The state banks will gradually be run as commercial banks that will compete for deposits with international banks.

When the stock market opened in the Astor, the city could draw on the expertise of only a dwindling group of octogenarians with the right experience. The Cultural Revolution left China short of a generation of qualified people. The universities were closed for nearly a decade, and it will take time for the generation who have gone abroad to study to return and mature. Shanghai's leaders are younger and better educated than in the past, but none of them properly understand capital markets or how they should work.

One day there will be professional managers running insurance

Shanghai is trying to re-create its former reputation as China's art capital in centers like the Mo Gan Shan Art Factory.

companies and investment funds. Yet a flourishing financial services sector also requires independent regulators and auditors and independent courts to enforce verdicts against individual wrongdoers. Investors need a more transparent political system and a supply of news from independent media to properly assess risk. This scenario will be possible only with profound changes to the country's legal system, and that outcome ultimately awaits serious political reforms.

So far Shanghai has done the easy bit, building a new physical infrastructure, but the city's success depends on creating new institutions and nurturing the right human capital. The concrete has been poured at a great rate, but political change in China is proceeding at a snail's pace.

Great cities like London, New York, and Tokyo are also great cultural centers full of media companies, publishing houses, theaters, and art galleries that attract intellectuals from all over the world. By the 1930s Shanghai was the intellectual center of China, where the best books were written and the best films made. In fact, in almost any field, the work of these directors, actors, writers, composers, and painters has not been rivaled by anything done since then.

The heavy hand of state censorship continues to stifle this creativity, but there is still plenty going on. One day I went to Moganshan Street and found that the No. 12 Wool-weaving Factory, which had laid off its 2,000 workers and closed down four years earlier, had been turned into a new art center, the Shanghai Creative Industry Clustering Park. It was bustling with activity as workers finished turning the workshops into art galleries. A poster pasted onto many walls advertised the slogan "Shanghai Fashion Night—City—Culture—Memory."

First I stopped to chat with Wu Koutian, a 90-year-old retired worker. He was sitting outside some 1920s-era housing, a row of small shops beneath a red wood fronting. Behind him in a narrow alley was the house where Mr. Wu had lived for 60 years ever since he joined the flour mill, one of 12 factories nearby that had all belonged to the Rong family. The factories had all gone, replaced by a cluster of 30 pencil-thin apartment towers painted in shades of gray and green.

"My house will be demolished any day soon. Who knows?" grumbled Mr. Wu. "Everyone else who lived here has already gone." Only foreigners could afford to pay 10,000 renminbi ("people's currency"; $1,250) per square foot to live in one of the flats. Yet Shanghai does have a middle class who can afford to buy cars, new houses, insurance policies, and expensive foreign holidays. I wondered if they were yet buying modern art.

At the Traveled Coffee and Tea bar, I chatted with a girl who had arrived from Wenzhou in Zhejiang Province a few months earlier and was now deftly serving dark espressos and wearing heavy eye shadow. She thought Shanghai was at least seven years behind Beijing and other cities. The Shanghai Creative Industry Clustering Park looked like a copy of Beijing's No. 798 Factory, where the avant-garde has taken over part of an electronics factory complex built by East Germans in the 1950s.

In the 1920s and 1930s, Shanghai had been at the cutting edge of all modern art, music, and literature. The Shanghai film industry was the biggest in Asia and it exerted a profound influence on the morals, fashions, and lifestyles that the young sought to emulate. Mao's fourth wife, Jiang Qing, was a Shanghai starlet in the 1930s who later took charge of the arts in the Cultural Revolution, turned it into a propaganda tool, and destroyed the lives of all her old associates. Chinese popular films began to be made in Hong Kong, which turned its kung fu flicks into a global success. Hong Kong still has the best and freest media in the Chinese world.

Yet there is no doubt that Shanghai is still the city of dreams for every Chinese, rich or poor. It is where everybody still heads to realize their hopes. At an upscale furniture store, I found an actor friend, Liu Linian, making a new film, a bittersweet comedy about contemporary life. The female lead, played by Siqing Gaowang, is working as a model for a company selling water mattresses. She is one of the "educated youths" who were expelled from Shanghai during the Cultural Revolution and sent to the Great Northern Wilderness bordering the Soviet Union. She stays on there and gets married.

Liu's character is an old college classmate of hers, and one day Siqing's character hears on TV that he has retired and gone on a cycling tour around the world. It makes her think that she, too, ought be getting more out of life so she returns to Shanghai. There she tries to take up where her old life had left off. "The trouble is she can't get used to the new way of life in Shanghai," Liu explained. "She soon finds that she doesn't have enough money to really enjoy anything in Shanghai." Shanghai is now, as the film shows, a city reserved for the wealthy, or at least for the young.

The film's director, Anne Hoi, came from Hong Kong and it was being produced and financed by a Hong Kong company that wanted to make use of Shanghai's cheap nonunionized labor. Shanghai's own film studios produce just a handful of feature films a year and, despite the international awards won by Chinese actresses and directors, have still not recovered. "The talent is just not here anymore. It has moved to Beijing. The writers and directors are all there," Liu said. "Maybe one day Shanghai will get it back."

Some other aspects of old Shanghai are, however, very visibly back in force, like beggars and prostitutes. "Just something to eat," pleaded an old peasant woman on Huaihai Road, thrusting forward a four-year-old, far too young to be her own son, who stumbled forward holding a broken plastic disposable cup. "We are Anhui peasants who lost our land in last year's floods. Please give a little."

Child beggars are back on Shanghai's streets pestering the shoppers browsing the fashion boutiques on Nanjing Road and Huaihai Road and embarrassing revelers as they leave the nightclubs in their chauffeur-driven BMWs and Mercedes.

If you take the pedestrian underpass on the Bund, you pass a line of grotesquely disfigured humanity that supports itself by demanding alms. Some belong to the thousands of migrant workers who have been injured in industrial accidents or on building sites. Shanghai's reinvented modernity was achieved by importing nearly four million peasants to work around-the-clock in the construction boom.

Most beggars, especially those with young children, claim to come from the same five places in China that they did in the past, such as Fengyang in Anhui Province or Huiyang in Hunan Province. One elder-

ly beggar from Fengyang whom I spoke to on the entrance steps of the Astor Hotel first blamed his misfortunes on natural disaster but then changed his story. "Actually, it's my leg," he said, suddenly walking away with a heavy limp.

In the 1930s, Shanghai had 50,000 beggars, and the British, French, Americans, and others who ran the international concessions never worked out how to deal with them. According to legend, they were organized into eight leagues ruled by a beggar king who traced his ancestry way back to the Ming dynasty. The beggar chiefs negotiated with gangsters and foreign capitalists, allocated begging patches, and prevented turf wars. These beggars were even supposed to be patriotic by supporting such movements as the May 1919 protests.

Shanghai and other cities are debating new ordinances to deal with the beggars. For years the police could detain and arrest anyone with a peasant ID card and, if they had no written permission to be in the city, send them to a work camp. After this law was changed, the Shanghai police began creating a special task force to deal with the problem. The media have been reporting on the tricks used by beggars, such as Shanghai's own version of Fagin, 36-year-old Bao Wulian. He recruited a gang of small children aged 6 to 12 to pick pockets and snaffle mobile phones and wallets until he was arrested.

It is a peculiar aspect of China's reforms that it is still far easier to open a brothel than a church, a synagogue, or even a temple. Prostitution had been another symbol of all that was wrong with republican China. Shanghai was described as a Babylon, a "corrupt, pleasure mad, and squalor ridden city" with 100,000 prostitutes. As one writer, Stella Dong, put it, "The sickly sweet smell of opium permeated every lane and side street, and in its myriad fleshpots laboured a tragic army of prostitutes and 'taxi dancers.'"

When the Red Army marched into Shanghai in 1949, they arrested the prostitutes and other social parasites and sent them to camps to be reeducated in socialist morality and to acquire more useful skills. Some reformed girls acted out their escape from degradation on stage to scenes of mass hysteria from the assembled audience of students.

As American academic Gail Hershatter notes in her book *Dangerous Pleasures: Prostitution and Modernity in Twentieth-Century Shanghai*, "Sex

Despite—or because of— the renaissance of business and opportunity in Shanghai, beggars are ubiquitous on its streets.

work was taken as paradigmatic of a social decay that was then evoked to explain China's position vis-à-vis the colonizing powers."

From then until 1990, the "city without night" lacked a single private bar. The most decadent entertainment in Shanghai was an octogenarian jazz band that played 1930s hits in the old Cathay Hotel. But the Shanghai of today now boasts exclusive businessmen's clubs, trendy yuppie bars, private "KTV rooms" where you hire the girls by the hour, and thousands of massage parlors and "barbershops."

A short walk away from the Astor Hotel, I found a whole street of girls sitting in brightly neon-lit parlors watching TV, playing cards, and knitting. One of them, Wang Ping, a busty 30-year-old wearing a pink dress over fishnet stockings, told me about her life. She had come to Shanghai two months earlier from a small town in Heilongjiang Province. The state-owned factories had closed down and there was no work. She now lived a strange existence, never leaving the brothel, but would soon be heading home. "In another few months, I will have enough savings to open a children's clothes shop back home and can quit this work," she said.

In the 1920s the Shanghai Municipal Council came up with a plan to license brothels and gradually restrict the number of licenses issued until there were none left. Needless to say, it didn't work, but the subject has become topical again. Sociology professor Pan Suiming from the University of China in Beijing, who spent seven years researching prostitution, regards it as an inevitable part of the economic reforms and suggests legalizing the practice. Some cities in China have already begun licensing the industry by issuing special work permits or levying taxes. "The biggest problem in the sex industry is that it is illegal," he says. "That means women fall under the control of pimps and criminal gangs because they turn to them to find clients."

It took not much more than a decade for this particular wheel in Shanghai to come full circle. In a way, it is a reason for optimism that all those areas where progress is absent, like intellectual freedom, will eventually see a similar restoration. The city was once the foremost center for higher education in China, home to 39 universities, including St. John's College, founded in 1879 by American Protestants, and Tongji University, established by Germans in 1907.

Shanghai's booming nightlife ranges from go-go clubs to seamier establishments in a city where prostitution is rife.

Shanghai's future really rests on software, creating the right intellectual capital to support its aspirations to move away from labor-intensive manufacturing and to become a center for financial and high-tech industries. To do so, it must attract the brightest minds in the country. Salaries are still so low that the universities have trouble attracting and keeping top academics. Many of the leading universities have, however, built new campuses and student residence halls outside the city. A new immigration policy grants residency to any students graduating in the right fields even if they were not born in Shanghai. (To fill up the empty high-rises, the city was also offering residency to outsiders willing to spend a million yuan, later revised down to 400,000 yuan, on buying a property.)

Many of the new campuses cluster around a satellite town called Songjiang. One afternoon I hired a taxi and drove out to see it. After an hour speeding along a highway past paddy fields, factories, and villa parks, we reached Songjiang. The town had been built in the Ming dynasty and once had a city wall. It also was known for its picturesque old railway station, which was often featured in movies set in the 1930s.

There was now no trace of the old railway station, let alone any Ming dynasty buildings. It was an entirely new city. Work was under way on a giant new railway terminus that will house the biggest shopping mall in China, with a floor space of more than three million square feet. A new rail link will cut the journey time from Shanghai to about 15 minutes.

Around Songjiang, I found a host of new buildings eclectically designed in a range of styles from the ultramodern to a nouveau Renaissance complete with cupolas and Greek pillars. Nine universities, with 100,000 students and staff, are being relocated here.

It was unnerving to find this architecture plonked in the middle of the Yangtze Delta—but even more surprising to find a complete English country town being re-created. This was a real estate development called Thamestown that included a pub with oak beams by the waterside, flagstone streets, and Georgian terraces. The mock-Tudor village houses were surrounded by suburban streets with Edwardian villas lined by London plane trees and yew and hawthorn hedges. There were football pitches, a garden maze, shops, schools, and a lake. The whole effect was crowned by a full-size replica of an Anglican church with a pointed slate steeple.

I left Songjiang and Thamestown bewildered. Shanghai was busy bulldozing its wonderful architectural heritage, including some authentic Edwardian houses, and here it was being re-created. Thamestown was only one of eight new satellite towns that the government had invited foreign architects from Germany, Holland, Italy, and Sweden to create. Few people had yet started living in Thamestown, but the houses were said to be selling fast, although no one in the sales office seemed to be sure what was to become of the church.

The Shanghainese have always flattered themselves that, as China's greatest window on the world, they are the most modern and most receptive to foreign things. Yet the architecture seems more to speak of the great power of nostalgia and a hunger for a lost past.

China looks for its high-tech future to come from graduates such as these, in Shanghai's newly created university town of Songjiang.

THE NORTHEAST

THE SOVIET INDUSTRIAL LEGACY

CHAPTER THREE

T he smokestacks had gone. The air felt fresher. In place of grimy factories, there were now fancy car showrooms, new apartment blocks in pastel shades, and neon-lit shopping malls. I hardly recognized Shenyang, the rusting capital of China's state-owned enterprises (SOEs). On my previous visits, it had seemed forever caught in some 1930s black-and-white newsreel footage of the Great Depression. Sullen workers dressed in overcoats emerged from shabby tenements coated in coal dust to loiter in the parks or gather in front of government buildings to stage muted protests demanding back wages and unpaid pensions.

When I first came here 20 years ago, the dispiriting miasma of pollution and decay seemed to fix the capital of Liaoning Province forever in the past. Oversize concrete statues of Chairman Mao Zedong, his hand raised in greeting at statues of proud workers with the bulging muscles of superheroes, all recalled the heyday of the 1960s when the Northeast was the future of China.

China's high economic-growth rates, averaging 10 percent per annum, have masked a puzzle. The statistics seem to show that China managed better than the Soviet Union and Eastern Europe by attracting investment and creating tens of millions of new jobs. Yet the truth is that the Chinese could not and did not escape the vast and painful dislocation that followed the collapse of communism elsewhere.

The decline of the SOEs accelerated in the 1990s as giant Soviet-

Chairman Mao Zedong remains as prominent as ever in Northeast China despite the modernization of Chinese culture.

PREVIOUS PAGES
A man works at a tire factory. Heavy industry has been the lifeblood of Northeast China since the large-scale industrialization of the early 1950s.

style factories went bankrupt and closed down, throwing more than half the labor force out of work. In Liaoning Province, five million out of ten million workers lost their jobs in state factories by 1997. Some 31.4 million SOE workers were laid off across the country between 1996 and 2000, and in total the figure may now run to more than 45 million people. Huge swaths of smokestack industry collapsed into bankruptcy, causing widespread poverty in urban China.

One of China's greatest challenges has been to find a way of reviving its heavy industry and saving as much as possible of the old state sector. It has been a remarkable story. In places like Shenyang, one can see the first signs of success, but, as this chapter explains, the social and financial cost has been so great that at times it has endangered Deng Xiaoping's entire modernization project.

When the Soviet Union was China's big brother in the 1950s,

it helped create an industrial economy that eventually rivaled the big brother's in size. China's centrally planned economy was not a failure, at least when measured against its own standard. Giant vertically integrated enterprises produced as much iron, coal, and other heavy industrial commodities as the Soviet Union. They employed more than 100 million people, including those working in the schools, hospitals, and other welfare services that served these SOEs. The most massive of these enterprises, like the steel works in Anshan, about 100 miles from Shenyang in Liaoning Province, employed more than 400,000 people. And most of these people enjoyed a secure job and high standard of living.

Just as in the Soviet Union, much of this great investment in heavy industry was designed to support a gigantic military expansion. China created a military-industrial complex that by some measures ranks among the greatest in the world. By the 1970s, the People's Liberation Army (PLA) possessed 10,000 battle tanks, 5,000 military aircraft, and the world's largest fleet, and it was furiously building more. In the 1970s, the Chinese were still erecting new giant factories, like Factory No. 5419 (all the factories were known by numbers), which I once visited. This huge industrial complex had been constructed in the middle of nowhere, hidden in obscure valleys southwest of Beijing on the border of Shaanxi and Hebei Provinces, and was designed to produce the steel, engines, and other parts to assemble a staggering 2,500 tanks a year.

Northeast China was known as Manchuria before 1949 because it was the homeland to the Manchus who conquered China in the 17th century. Until the end of the 19th century, most of this area was off-limits to Chinese migration, and it remained thinly populated by Mongol and Manchu nomads. The region beyond the Great Wall had rich untapped resources of coal, iron ore, timber, and hydroelectric power. When the Japanese in the 1930s conquered Manchuria after occupying Korea, they planned to turn it into a great colony in which tens of millions of Japanese would settle.

When the Japanese went home after 1945, they left behind a well-developed infrastructure of dams, factories, roads, and railways. Joseph Stalin, whose troops had occupied the region, was reluctant to

The Soviet-built electrical power plant in the background signaled the future for the Manchurian town of Fushun in 1947.

hand Manchuria over to the People's Republic of China, and even after 1949 toyed with the idea of creating a buffer state. In the end Manchuria became neither a Japanese nor a Russian colony; instead, the new government of China settled tens of millions of migrants from central and eastern China there during the 1950s. The three provinces of the Northeast—Liaoning, Jilin, and Heilongjiang—are now home to 110 million people.

After 1949, Moscow built 156 major industrial complexes in China, one of the biggest technology transfers in history, and the Northeast, close to the Soviet border and linked by the Trans-Siberian railway originally built in tsarist times, was a favored location. Most of the Russian-style buildings have disappeared, but the Soviet mentality left a deeper impression here than anywhere else.

In fact, central planning was more rigorously applied in China than the Soviet Union. Chinese factory managers had even less room for initiative than anywhere else in the socialist world. Everything was minutely regulated according to a plan set by one of the hundred-plus ministries in Beijing. The workers lucky enough to be employed by these factories were guaranteed an "iron rice bowl," which meant they could never be fired however lazy or incompetent they might be. In the 1990s, a World Bank survey of five industrial cities in China concluded that Shenyang workers had the worst record of labor productivity and were only half as productive as those in Shanghai.

In some respects the post-1949 development of Manchuria's empty steppes and forests bears many similarities to Stalin's great project to colonize Siberia. Both depended on transporting political prisoners to work in labor camps to tame a wilderness and to build large industrial complexes. Some historians now think the attempt to settle the huge white spaces of Siberia was such an ambitious endeavor and brought such poor returns that it ultimately destroyed the Soviet economy. Since the Soviet Union collapsed, millions of people have left Siberia and gone back to live in European Russia.

Similarly, China sent more than 100,000 troops to Heilongjiang Province to start the colonization of what was called the Great Northern Wilderness. They were joined by millions of political prisoners and educated youths from the cities who were settled in large labor

Preparing for the possibility of nuclear war, China built underground cities in Harbin, shown here, and elsewhere, comprising bombproof factories for vital industries, plus dormitories, dining halls, warehouses, and hospitals.

camps. They felled trees, drained marshes, and built roads. The discovery of oil in the Daqing oil fields in Heilongjiang in 1959, enough to help keep China self-sufficient until the early 1990s, spurred further migration. Heilongjiang produced half of China's petroleum, 40 percent of its timber, and one-third of its heavy industrial machinery. For a long time, the settlement of the Northeast was a great boon to China's economy. Yet half a century later, the forests had been felled, the coal and iron ore mines were exhausted, the oil was declining, the machinery was outdated, and the profitability of the enterprises founded in the 1950s was eroded by the burden of supporting a large population of retirees.

In the 1960s, China prepared to fight a nuclear war with its elder brother and started to create a new military-industrial complex in the interior. This complex was called the "Third Line" and employed some 16 million people. Many new industrial complexes were created in remote mountainous areas, with the factories often being installed inside the mountains themselves. For this reason, pockets of what one might call SOE settlements can be found all over China's interior. In this respect, these enterprises share the post-1990 problems of many factories in the Soviet Union, which were scattered across the vast empire far from their suppliers and customers.

Soviet planners began moving factories east in 1941 in response to the German invasion. Chairman Mao and his right-hand man, Marshal Lin Biao, who ran the PLA, also scattered industry across the country for strategic reasons. Mao believed that in this way China would be able to continue fighting even after a Soviet nuclear attack and invasion. Some recent research also claims that Mao's military buildup was not only defensive but also aggressive and that he had dreams of world conquest. Certainly, the Chinese factories also churned out weapons freely given to Chinese allies across Africa and Asia.

In the Cold War global arms race, China could compete in quantity but not in quality. Its armaments relied heavily on technology transferred from the Soviet Union in the 1950s. Some of that technology was actually from Nazi Germany, taken by the Soviets after World War II. China managed to build rockets and nuclear weapons, but its tanks and aircraft increasingly belonged in a museum rather than on

Many of China's industries stagnated for decades, as illustrated by the continued use of steam locomotives.

the battlefield. Even though the PLA employed some 300,000 scientists and technicians, the technology gap widened in the 1950s. China's costly efforts to develop its own technology did not produce the modern fighter jets or nuclear-powered submarines that it wanted. One major hindrance was the Cultural Revolution, which saw universities closed, the outside world shut off, and the intelligentsia persecuted and sent off to do farm labor in the countryside. China missed out on the whole electronics revolution.

Before his death in 1976, Mao came to distrust Lin Biao, whom he suspected of trying to assassinate him and usurp power. Lin and his family died in mysterious circumstances as they attempted to flee to the Soviet Union. As Mao slipped into senility before his death, Deng

Xiaoping was brought back into power and began to slow defense spending. As he strengthened his grip on power, Deng canceled all the big defense procurement orders and began to demobilize on a grand scale. The military's train lines, airfields, harbors, coal mines, and steel plants, and the many military factories that made everything from clothes to medicines, began to be transferred into civilian hands.

The defense factories were told to switch to producing civilian goods, to make tractors instead of tanks. The military was effectively ordered to go into business, and this they did. In 1993, the CIA estimated that the profits of "PLA Inc." topped five billion dollars a year. The impact of the dislocation was also partly softened by the Iran-Iraq war between 1980 and 1988. The two sides, rich in oil, created a huge market for just the kind of hardware that the Chinese produced cheaply.

Even so, most SOEs began to lose money as the domestic orders dried up. When China opened the doors to imports and foreign investors entered the market, state factories found it harder and harder to stay afloat. By the late 1990s, two-thirds of all defense factories were operating in the red. Those factories making textiles and machine tools that competed with foreign-invested factories in the south lost their customers and depended on ever larger subsidies to stay afloat. Few factories managed the transition to the consumer market. Without the transfer of profits from SOEs, central government revenues shrank until they accounted for just 11 percent of gross domestic product.

When the Soviet Union was formally dissolved in 1992, its military-industrial complex accounted for more than a quarter of the economy. Its factories had a supply chain scattered across a huge territory, and if they could not find new customers or products, they quickly had to close down. Civilian factories had similar problems. The big textile mills, for instance, depended on cotton delivered by suppliers that were now in separate and independent states such as Uzbekistan and free to sell to anyone at a market price. As the centrally planned economy disintegrated, the economies of all the former states of the Soviet empire began to contract rapidly. When the new governments had no money to pay wages, the workforces went on strike.

Much the same process took place in China after 1990. Beijing stopped setting the prices of raw materials and end products, and every plant was free to negotiate its own deal with suppliers and buyers. The complex web of interdependent factories quickly unraveled. The whole supply chain seized up, creating a chain of unpaid debts. Soon the SOEs owed each other 900 billion yuan of what were called "triangular debts."

Some blame the chaos in the former Soviet Union on the "shock therapy" advocated by free-market economists. In the new Russia, the postcommunist state sought a quick privatization of industry by issuing workers vouchers that could be traded like shares. The project went wrong and Russia defaulted on its debts in the 1998 financial crisis. In the economic meltdown, Russians were flooded by a nostalgia for the security of the good old days under Stalin and Leonid Brezhnev, when the state would reliably pay workers, miners, teachers, and soldiers on time. Some blamed capitalism for the pervasive lawlessness, the power of the mafia, and the excessive wealth of the new tycoons.

To many both in Russia and China, China seemed to have done the right thing by rejecting "shock therapy" and refusing to quickly privatize the state industrial sector. When I first visited Shenyang in 1986, such a privatization was very much in the cards. Shenyang opened the first stock market in China, years before Shanghai reopened its stock market in the old Astor Hotel. In Shenyang I found a small office where traders gathered to look at a blackboard on which the shares of a handful of "joint stock companies" were chalked up. Shenyang had also been chosen to pioneer the new bankruptcy law. The Shenyang Fireproof Materials Factory was the first to close down, a matter of great shame. No one in the city dared give me directions or even admit to knowing where it was.

At the 13th Party Congress in 1987, the Chinese leadership called for sweeping reforms in the management of the state industrial sector. Professional managers would come in one door and the all-powerful party secretaries would leave through the other. However, conservative leaders had grave reservations about the wisdom of divorcing the party from its key constituency, the proletariat. Their caution was indicated in 1989. According to Marxist dogma, the party was the "advance guard of the proletariat," and in the face of huge student street protests in Shanghai, Beijing, and other cities, the party was able

to call on workers, arm them with sticks, and bring them onto the streets. The workers did not join the students.

After Tiananmen, the party decided that it would hold onto the state-owned enterprises but still reform them. SOEs were listed on the stock exchange but were not privatized. The workers were not issued tradable shares in their factories as they were in Russia (although this practice was tried in some places in China). Instead, the capital raised by the stock markets was used both to subsidize the state sector and to keep it in the hands of the party. By contrast, in Boris Yeltsin's Russia, the top priority of his economic advisers was to break the iron grip of the Soviet Communist Party over the society for good, an objective it achieved.

When generals sent tanks onto the streets of Moscow, the coup failed.

In China, the approach was exactly the opposite. The Chinese Communist Party was determined to stay in power. The Chinese leaders during the 1990s had spent their careers in SOEs, and they were determined to save the SOEs no matter what the cost. Many were engineers who had been trained in Stalin's lifetime. Jiang Zemin, who had studied engineering in Shanghai, was sent to Moscow in the 1950s and worked at the Stalin automobile plant outside Moscow. On his return, he went to work for China's First Automobile Works in Changchun in Jilin Province, one of the giant industrial plants built by the Soviets. Its emblematic product was the Liberation truck, and the factory was still making it the same way when Jiang became president of China as it did 40 years earlier when he started work there. During his 12 years in power, state television often showed Jiang visiting a big state factory and leading workers in a sing-along with songs from the 1950s.

As the Chinese leadership wanted to prevent SOEs from going bankrupt, the bankruptcy law was suspended. This action meant that even if a state-owned factory were technically bankrupt, its workers would never be laid off. Instead, the state invented a huge variety of euphemisms to describe workers who had no work. A worker was not laid off but had *Xia Gang,* or stepped down from his post. His lack of employment or wage did not qualify him to be recorded in unemployment statistics. Shenyang, for example, regularly reported an unemployment rate of less than 5 percent, even when half the industrial workforce was out of work. The Chinese created a poetic word for the process. They described a factory that had gone bust as *huang le,* having "yellowed," like an autumn leaf. When you went around a place like Shenyang, people said this or that factory had yellowed with a hapless shrug of resignation. The shrug was supposed to tell you that this misfortune was just an unavoidable event that no one could stop.

China had about 300,000 state-owned enterprises, and more than a thousand of the largest enterprises were listed on the newly opened stock markets in Shanghai and Shenzhen. Other SOEs raised capital in Hong Kong and New York. Altogether, some 160 billion dollars was raised, but the state has provided much more money—giving enterprises interest-free loans, direct government handouts, and written-off

State-owned enterprises like this linen mill in Harbin once provided job security for life, but at a cost of poor productivity.

debts. In fact, the SOEs have absorbed 70 to 80 percent of the loans handed out by state banks.

Just how much of this money has been or will ever be recovered is anyone's guess. Whether the vast sums involved would have been better invested remains a question that is never publicly discussed in China. The accounting is just too murky for outside economists to be sure, but few doubt that the returns from investment in the SOEs have been poor.

By the mid-1990s, the net credit to SOEs reached more than 12 percent of GDP. The state banking system was burdened by 180 billion dollars of nonperforming loans, according to the government (or 450 billion dollars, if you believe various Western estimates).

The scale of China's SOE problem becomes even clearer if one draws a comparison with what has happened to East Germany's economy over the same period. Before the Berlin Wall fell in 1989, the German Democratic Republic was known as the most successful economy in the entire Soviet bloc. At one time East Germany was rated as the world's seventh largest industrial economy. Even though more than 1.5 trillion dollars have poured into East Germany, that sum has not been enough to save industry from disappearing. None of East Germany's enterprises survived the competition from West Germany, and the number of people in employment quickly dropped from almost ten million to about six million. Even in 2005, unemployment in East Germany stood at 17.8 percent with two million out of work. The region has been almost deindustrialized and many people have had to leave their homes to find employment.

Whenever I visited Shenyang, I wondered if it was fair to say that the Chinese had dealt with the problem better than the Russians or Germans. One person I met in Shenyang was Zhou Wei, a retired SOE factory manager. He was convinced that the vast sums being poured into the SOEs were being squandered, and he was leading a personal campaign against a sea of corruption. The local party organization treated him as a dangerous public enemy. The first time I came to visit him, the secret police, driving a BMW with blackened windows, tailed me from the airport. After elaborate measures to shake them off, we made our way to his tiny flat, piled with documents and crowded with his supporters.

Zhou spoke at length of his difficulties trying to reach over the heads of the Shenyang party committee to lobby the leadership in Beijing. His phones were bugged, his apartment watched around the clock. It was hard for him to leave Shenyang in secret without being caught; the police were watching for him at the bus and train stations. Once in Beijing Zhou and his companions had to hide in hotels and stash their documents under their beds for fear that the Shenyang police would find them and drag them back. Zhou was eventually arrested in 1999 and given a two-year administrative prison term in the Dragon Mountain Labor Reeducation Camp, charged with "reporting for the masses."

It struck me as odd that he was at once a supporter of the old centrally planned economy and a dissident in the new China. In fact, Zhou seemed to me slightly deranged in his faith in the Communist Party, so I discounted his allegations against leading officials. For example, he accused Mu Suixin, the mayor of Shenyang and a rising star, of involvement in an illegal pyramid scheme that had collapsed, wiping out the life savings of thousands of people. "Suddenly, we had a lot of billionaires in this town," he said bitterly.

Many laid-off workers had invested their redundancy money in semiprivate investment funds. One of them whom I met in Zhou's flat was Tian Yuzhu, a severe-looking woman with a dark shawl covering her head. Her family deposited 600,000 yuan into the Huaxia Fund run by Sun Yingqi, a high-ranking officer at the State Criminal Police College. Huaxia guaranteed annual dividends of 20 or 30 percent, and some 30,000 households invested their family savings into the fund.

Mrs. Tian showed me her deposit certificate and the fund's brochure with photos of Sun sitting at a desk in a police uniform. The prospectus said that the fund had investments in taxi firms and nightclubs in Shenyang, coal mines, pig farms, and a steel-trading venture in Lithuania. "The government registered this as a triple-A creditworthy enterprise," she said.

Sun Yingqi turned out to be an impostor who had nothing to do with the police, and in 1998 the Huaxia Fund was shut down on Beijing's orders during a campaign against such funds. What made

Mrs. Tian so suspicious was that just beforehand local law-enforcement officers tipped off Sun, who absconded to the United States with most of the cash. But was it possible that the corruption reached into the highest ranks of the city's leadership as Zhou alleged?

I had met Mayor Mu Suixin on one of his visits to Beijing. A tall, louche, chain-smoking graduate of Beijing's prestigious Qinghua University, he had a bullish charm. He spoke confidently of being able to restore the Shenyang's industry to profitability within three years, a deadline imposed in 1997 by then premier Zhu Rongji. Mayor Mu toured southern China and London, Rome, Paris, and Tokyo, trying to find buyers for his struggling factories, and he won attention by offering to sell them for a token one yuan. The offer interested many buyers, but they backed away when they found they had to shoulder the welfare burdens of providing for surplus workers and retirees' pensions. "They are waiting for a miracle here," was how Zhou Wei described it. "All the big factories are bankrupt." He thought Mu's schemes were enabling corrupt managers to strip the SOEs of their assets or privatize them at well below their market value in management buyout deals.

Mayor Mu's energetic lobbying did attract investment and massive reconstruction of the city and sometimes double-digit economic growth rates. In 1999, the United Nations even awarded him a prize for his efforts in improving Shenyang's housing. Under his leadership, Shenyang began demolishing the Tiexi industrial zone, with its factories and housing that dated from the Japanese occupation in the 1930s. Workers had enjoyed rent-free housing, but now as they moved into the new high-rises, they had to take out mortgages. The distinctive workers' housing, comfortable three-story blocks of red brick designed around open courtyards, had been built in the 1960s according to Soviet blueprints. Even though there was no need to knock them down, Shenyang officials had them demolished along with the much grimmer gray concrete blocks dating from the 1970s.

Much of the huge amount of money spent on reviving Shenyang had gone into this construction boom. It had changed the face of Shenyang, but Zhou argued that the money had been misspent or stolen. Most inhabitants, he said, were too poor to buy the new housing. By 1995, nearly 80 percent of the two million workers had been

A Shenyang school is imploded as the city continues its facelift.

laid off. They were paid just 129 yuan a month by their old factories, barely enough to live on, and some were getting as little as 15 yuan. Mayor Mu had dispatched hundreds of thousands of unemployed workers to the surrounding countryside to work in farming.

In addition, the city had 560,000 pensioners—but only one in five was actually receiving a pension. Consequently, Zhou insisted, 80 percent of the apartments were left empty and many of the real estate companies were going bust. Furthermore, many of the new buildings

hurriedly thrown up had used substandard building materials as the local mafia seized control of the construction industry.

Zhou went even further, declaring that the party *was* the mafia, and that, in fact, things were even worse in this respect than in the former Soviet Union. Shenyang had been notorious in precommunist days for being under the grip of organized criminal gangs. With Mayor Mu's blessing, according to Zhou, Shenyang gangsters had again taken over the economy, controlling construction, tobacco, gambling, prostitution, car smuggling, and the manufacture and export of drugs. The Northeast became flooded by amphetamine "ice" and ecstasy, known in the mainland as *yaotou wan* or the head-shaking drug.

The first to be laid off from state-owned factories was the female workforce. One of Mu's initiatives was to encourage the opening of bars and massage parlors. Soon there were tens of thousands of girls working in bars, nightclubs, and hotels. Mayor Mu even passed legislation offering work permits to women who registered and paid a 20 percent tax on their earnings. A month later he was forced to withdraw it, partly in response to protests by some in the underworld who felt it was cutting into their profits.

When Zhou was released from prison in 2001, he resolved to continue investigating the government corruption in Shenyang and finding ways to deliver evidence in petitions to central government leaders in Beijing. As it happened, the central government investigations were already well advanced. Party inspectors uncovered corruption on a scale even greater than Zhou had claimed, and the revelations brought down the entire municipal government.

When Mu was finally arrested in 2001, investigators searching his two country houses found six million dollars' worth of gold bars hidden in the walls, 150 Rolex watches, and computer files documenting years of corruption that infected almost every government department. A government report found that the mayor, his wife, daughter, and lover, his executive vice-mayor, the police, prosecutors, judges, customs officers, construction bureaus, private companies, bankers, and local legislators were all on the take.

Mu gave contracts to his daughter to improve Shenyang's lighting, and investigators found she had a bank account in Hong Kong containing three million dollars. When the city hired a Hong Kong construction company to build a highway around the city, Mu's wife Zhang Yafei stepped in and sold bad construction material to the project. Six months after the project was finished, the road was split open with potholes. Even in the middle of the investigation, Mu's wife was so powerful that she had managed to buy her husband's freedom for several months, and she had come close to quashing the probe.

The mayor's deputy, Ma Xiangdong, was even more shameless. He drove a red Ferrari and was finally caught gambling in Macao. He had been there 12 times and also to Las Vegas and had gambled away four million dollars in public funds.

One of Shenyang's most successful businessmen was a gangster, Liu Yong, who built up a major conglomerate, the Jiayang Group, which worked hand in glove with Mayor Mu's government, and who was appointed a legislator in the local People's Congress. Later Liu, a slightly built man with a violent temper, was accused of 40 murders, mostly of people who lived on property that his real estate firm wanted to develop and who refused to leave. He also ran convenience stores and construction companies using migrant laborers, and he smuggled cars and drugs from North Korea.

Liu had long been protected by his brother, a senior police officer, and by Shenyang's top procurator, Liu Shi, a family friend but not a relative. Liu was caught in July 2000 trying to escape to Russia and then attempted to commit suicide with sleeping pills. He was eventually tried and shot after being convicted of multiple counts of tax evasion, assault, possession of firearms, extortion, kidnapping, and the murder of a tobacco vendor working in the city without Liu's permission.

In the crackdown, more than 800 officials were arrested and 120 leading officials were charged for activities that ran from smuggling to buying and selling official positions, stealing farmland for big development projects, rigging construction contracts, and embezzling government funds. Mayor Mu was eventually given a suspended death sentence, but Zhou was also arrested again and charged with fomenting unrest.

Perhaps the most remarkable part of this story, given the scale of the corruption and the extent of the unemployment, is what did *not* happen. No major workers' uprising has taken place in the Northeast, although the Communist Party has long feared the emergence of a Chinese equivalent of Poland's Solidarity Movement. All across the Northeast, there has been plenty of unrest. Workers have staged factory sit-ins and gathered to protest outside government offices. Often workers have blocked railway lines—sometimes for weeks on end—when they had not been paid. Yet none of these protests became politicized.

One of the most serious uprisings took place in Liaoyang, about 62 miles east of Shenyang, in spring 2002. A protest led by laid-off workers at a ferro-alloy plant, one of the city's largest state-owned enterprises, quickly spread to other factories after the police detained the labor leaders. Soon there were 30,000 workers on the streets. It coincided with protests by thousands of workers at the Daqing oil fields in Heilongjiang Province who were angered by paltry redundancy payments. But again, this protest did not lead to political action.

To find out why, I went back to Liaoyang three years after the strikes had been suppressed. An industrial city of 1.6 million, Liaoyang is just a small version of Shenyang. It had a big textile factory that had "yellowed" ten years earlier and 5,000 workers lost their jobs. Among them was Qu Shuiping, who drove me around in his taxi. He described how it happened: "We used to have the highest living standards in the country. It all started to go wrong with Deng's reforms." It was competition from new factories that opened in the south that put them out of business. "Who can compete with migrant laborers in the south who work twice as many hours for half the money?" he said. The factory dated back to the 1950s. Even the weaving machinery, gathering dust on the empty work floor, was so old nobody could be found to buy it.

"When [the factory] closed, we were all given twenty thousand yuan. They said, 'We won't ask anything of you, and you don't bother us anymore.'" Soon afterward, the town's other big employer, a PLA arms factory, also went bust, throwing another 5,000 out of work.

The third big enterprise in Liaoyang was the ferro-alloy plant, a sprawling compound of chimneys and rail tracks that employed 6,000 people. This enterprise was an example of how often efforts to turn around the SOEs went sour. In 1995 the party installed a new official, Fan Yicheng, to act as both party secretary and director of the plant.

Many workers at SOEs in the Northeast like this coal miner have lost jobs and pensions due to corruption and mismanagement.

Together with the party secretary of Liaoyang, Gong Shangwu, Fan worked out a rescue strategy that included spinning off several production lines into independent companies.

Six years later, the Liaoyang government formally declared the ferro-alloy factory insolvent. Shortly afterward, several constituent parts of the factory were sold off to contractors who had close personal links to Fan and various local government leaders. Nearly the entire workforce was laid off and the promised redundancy packages were never paid, nor were pensions. Most workers received instead a monthly subsistence allowance of 182 yuan.

The workers found out that when Fan took control of the factory in 1995, he had halted fresh contributions to the plant's pension and medical funds, so there was now a shortfall of 27 million yuan. Furthermore, the workers had wondered where Fan got the money to support his lavish lifestyle, which

included paying for his children to study abroad. They found evidence that he had embezzled more than 100 million yuan and accused Gong Shangwu of being Fan's accomplice.

For three years the workers wrote letters and delivered petitions to Jiang Zemin:

> Respected and beloved General Secretary Jiang, we do not oppose the leadership of the party or the socialist system. Aside from demanding our legitimate and legal rights, all

our efforts were aimed to help the country dig out and eliminate all the corrupt worms boring away at and ruining our socialist economic system. The Liaoyang government used violent suppression against us while corruption was glossed over, leaving nearly all of us wondering and perplexed. Where on this earth are we to go to find reason and justice? Is it possible that a Chinese nation under the leadership of the Communist Party can leave no space for workers?

Then, when Gong Shangwu went to Beijing and appeared on national television boasting that in Liaoyang the unemployment problem had been basically solved and that all unemployed workers were receiving a minimum monthly payment of 280 yuan, their anger boiled over and they took to the streets. An investigation started and revealed that the workers' worst suspicions were well founded. Fan was arrested and sentenced to 13 years for corruption. Most of the senior management were also punished with stiff sentences.

News of the protests was kept out of the state media to prevent them from spreading. Police detained and expelled foreign journalists who arrived to cover the unrest. The authorities refused to open the company books and make public the evidence against the corrupt managers or party officials. Instead, the police arrested labor leaders like Yao Fuxin and gave them lengthy prison terms for organizing "illegal assembly, marches, and protests." China later brushed off appeals on behalf of Yao. The International Confederation of Free Trade Unions lodged a formal complaint at the International Labor Organization's Committee on Freedom of Association over the arrest of Yao, but to little effect.

It is telling that the workers' protest movement quickly collapsed. The government placated some with cash handouts and intimidated others with a threatening police presence and meting out exemplary harsh punishments to the braver voices. It is also revealing how, in their appeal to Jiang Zemin, former SOE workers still felt loyal to the Communist Party and expected it to help them. Decades of dependence on the state bred a passive attitude that some Chinese experts say is partly to blame for the workers' plight.

As Ou Xinqian, a senior official with the National Development and Reform Commission, put it, the Northeast must undergo "a total change of mind-set" and needs to escape the mentality bred of decades of Soviet-style economic planning. The region needs to develop a keen commercial sense and only the infusion of private capital could foster "a highly competitive, fully energetic business environment." Increasingly, the solution to the area's problems is seen as privatization. More and more of the factories and mines of the Northeast have been contracted out to private owners.

The private sector, especially the service sector, has been able to create new jobs. Liaoyang and other cities are full of new shops and restaurants. Liaoyang has a number of profitable and growing new private companies including the Fu Hao, one of the country's largest soybean-oil enterprises.

In the past decade, the number of enterprises across China still owned by the state has been cut in half to 150,000. Many of the factories have been sold off or leased to private businessmen. A few have been officially declared bankrupt. Between 1996 and 2000, bankruptcy claimed some 5,300 SOEs, resulting in 25 billion dollars in loan write-offs.

The central government responded to the 2002 worker unrest by increasing public infrastructure spending. In the following year it unveiled a "Revitalize the Northeast" plan and a list of one hundred "important projects" with a price tag of 61 billion yuan (7.3 billion dollars). The money was to come in the form of low-interest loans from state-owned banks, supplemented by capital from foreign investors and other sources, in part to further reform and privatize SOEs.

The province hopes to revitalize the industrial sector by focusing on the development of seven basic industrial sectors: shipbuilding, automobile production, transportation infrastructure, equipment manufacturing, steel, petrochemicals, and pharmaceuticals. More than half of the projects and 73 percent of the investment will go to Liaoning, the biggest province. The projects consist mainly of upgrading SOEs in such sectors as equipment manufacturing, raw-materials production, and food processing, but Liaoning's big steel and shipbuilding plants will also benefit.

Not all the money has been wasted. Shenyang now has a new airport, improved highways, and an entirely rebuilt city center. The air is much cleaner after around three billion dollars was spent on environmental projects after 2002. Some 3,000 chimneys and smokestacks are gone.

Yet some of the investment has gone to some bizarre and questionable projects like Holland Village, an eye-catching real estate development as strange as Thamestown outside Shanghai. This 545-acre site is full of villas, apartment towers, and dining and entertainment centers set in a fantasy of 17th-century Holland, with step-gabled housing rising along a copy of Amsterdam's famous Herrenkracht. Inside one of the grandiose buildings, I found guests ushered past mock Vermeers and caught a glimpse of a pianist in coattails seated at a grand piano surrounded by red tulips. Amid the canals, windmills, tulips, and black swans, I wandered in astonishment around copies of such landmark buildings as the Amsterdam Railway Station and The Hague's Huis ten Bosch royal palace and International Court of Justice. There was even a full-scale copy of a Dutch sailing vessel.

Holland Village was the brainchild of Yang Bin, once rated as China's second richest man and photographed in front of his Rolls-Royce and two Mercedes-Benz limousines before he was arrested and given an 18-year sentence for corrupt business practices. Yang had studied in Holland and on his return went into business that included greenhouse horticulture and flower growing, especially tulips, for export.

In other places, the changes I observed were striking. The Dabei Labor Camp that once housed 160,000 inmates, who worked in prison factories making boots, shoes, soap, and cosmetics, had disappeared. Where there had once been grim blocks of buildings behind high brick walls topped by barbed wire, a dozen luxury apartment towers set in gardens were being built. All trace of the labor camp was gone; the prisoners had been relocated to a modern-looking prison farm about 20 miles outside the city.

The giant Shenyang steel plant had gone. The Tiexi No. 4 Rubber Products Factory, the Daily Chemical Materials Factory, the rechargeable battery plant, and all the other factories I had been to on previous visits had vanished. The only still-thriving SOE that I recog-

The restructuring of the economy has led to the opening of new retail outlets such as this shopping center in Harbin.

nized was the PLA's Red Dawn Factory. The cancellation of orders for tanks and airplanes had led to the dismissal of half its 20,000 workers by the mid-1990s. Yet the factory had survived, although it had changed its name to the Shenyang Avionics Company. It was again building aircraft engines with a full order book, but many of the workers had not been rehired.

By the end of the Mao era, China's military aviation industry had built up the capacity to produce as many as a thousand planes a year. After the first Gulf War, China had shelved its own efforts to design and build new models; it bought Sukhoi-27 supersonic aircraft from Russia and tried to buy electronic surveillance AWACS technology from Israel. The only technologies in its military-industrial sector that have proven successful are missile production and satellite manufacturing. China now has an ambitious program of manned space exploration and has built up a flourishing business in commercial satellite launches.

China's double-digit budget increases in defense spending after 1996 has helped a recovery in the defense sector and a return to profitability. Shenyang has been a key beneficiary, developing engines for a new fighter jet and for passenger planes. China never managed to produce its own commercial airliners and instead has become a major market for Boeing and Airbus. It now hopes to launch its own short-haul and midsize passenger jets onto the market.

The revival of defense spending has helped Shenyang's economy, but so has foreign investment. On the outskirts of the city, new factories have sprung up and many of them bear the names of Japanese, South Korean, American, and German multinational companies. The South Korean presence is especially visible in numerous shop and restaurant signs. Many major American companies, including General Motors, Goodyear, Pfizer, Cargill, and Amway, have invested in Liaoning. The Northeast attracted just four billion dollars from China's total of 52.7 billion dollars of foreign direct investment in 2002, less than the city of Shanghai. There is now talk of a real industrial renaissance taking root in the Northeast, though. Foreign investment in Shenyang alone reached a record high of 2.5 billion dollars in 2005.

The future of car manufacturing in the Northeast seems assured, with BMW committed to a 160-million-dollar joint venture with

Brilliance, a state-controlled company in Shenyang, to produce classic saloon cars. Volkswagen also has a 50 percent stake in a substantial car-making joint venture in Jilin with First Automobile Works. Even so, Liaoning Province has gone from being the pacesetter in industry and technology to 11th place in terms of provincial GDP. And the entire economy of the Northeast, with more than 100 million people, is no bigger than that of superrich Guangdong Province.

The biggest lift for the Northeast came on the heels of the Asian financial crisis that started in 1997. Even the *Worker's Daily* was calling the SOEs a "bottomless pit" in 1997 and reporting that their debts totaled four trillion yuan. As the economies of China's neighbors went into a tailspin, China's economy shrank and some 30 million jobs were lost. The then premier Zhu Rongji responded with a "trillion-dollar" infrastructure and public works program. At his final press conference when he stepped down five years later, Premier Zhu said that he saved China from "catastrophe." The results are visible everywhere in China in the shape of new highways, airports, ports, and, most of all, in the reconstruction of all Chinese cities. The vast spending program backed by special government bonds lifted the fortunes of China's heavy industries, including the state coal mines.

Until the public-works spending program started, planners assumed there would be no growth in steel, cement, and aluminum industries and, therefore, demand for coal would drop. In 1995 Beijing decided that no more electric power plants needed to be built for the next three years because electricity output would grow by no more than 4 percent a year. The central government started closing down privately or locally operated coal mines as the state-planning commission feared a costly surplus of electricity capacity. Domestic coal production had expanded from 560 million tons in 1980 to 1.4 billion tons in 1996, but it fell to 900 million in 1999. Yet within three years, output had doubled to reach 1.8 billion tons of coal, more than twice as much coal as the United States, the world's second largest coal producer. New studies suggest that with China's GDP growing so rapidly, its annual coal production could easily reach more than three billion tons by 2020, something no one thought could happen before 2050.

Across the Northeast, once bankrupt coal mines sprang back into life. Wages and pensions were paid again. Prices rocketed upward as electricity shortages plagued eastern China, causing many factories to halt production. As coal demand jumped so quickly and unexpectedly, the rail system, 60 percent of which is tied up in coal transport, struggled to cope and the whole transport system seized up. Even coal-mining provinces like Shaanxi ran out of coal; its power stations stopped generating electricity when just a week's stockpile was left in the yards.

Caught up in crippling electricity shortages, China now embarked on a furious program of power-plant building. Across the country, the construction of 500 new coal-burning power stations started that will triple the energy produced by coal-fired power stations by 2015. Over the next 30 years half the world's new power capacity is to be built in China.

It was the same story with steel. China produced just 27 million tons in 1980, but after the infrastructure-spending program was launched, steel output tripled. In other words, in five years China added as much capacity as there is in the entire United States, the world's second largest steel producer. At its peak, the U.S. steel industry produced about 100 million tons, but China produced more than 360 million tons by 2005 in an industry where global capacity is just under one billion tons.

By 2004 China replaced Japan as the world's largest iron ore importer when it bought 208 million tons, up from 70 million tons in 2000. Furthermore, China now accounts for 40 percent of world demand for cement; 30 percent of aluminum; and 25 percent of zinc, copper, and wood pulp. As the railways could not transport so much ore to inland steel plants, 40 million tons piled up in Chinese ports.

The profits of major SOEs shot up, reaching 75 billion dollars in 2005—but were immediately reinvested in expansion. The state had by this time moved 168 billion dollars' worth of nonperforming loans off the books and put them into asset management companies. It had also borne most of the restructuring costs for enterprises, taking over responsibility for social obligations like schools, hospitals, and the costs associated with workers' unemployment and early retirement.

The transformation of the SOEs into huge and profitable capitalist semi-monopolies is best illustrated by the oil sector and the fate of the workers at the Daqing oil fields in Heilongjiang Province. Tens of thousands staged protests in 2002 at the same time as those in Liaoyang. Their employer is PetroChina, which is listed on the New York and Hong Kong stock exchanges with a value of 29 billion dollars and earns annual profits of more than 7 billion dollars. Its chairman is chauffeured around in a Bentley, and PetroChina has become a multinational with investments around the world. Since the listing, the company has laid off 86,000 of its 420,000 workers, mainly workers in their late 40s and early 50s. Each received a one-time payment of 4,100 yuan ($495) for each year of service, a much better deal than the 10,000-yuan one-time payments given to the Liaoyang workers. Even so, the Daqing oil

As China's public-works spending skyrockets, industry and its suppliers of energy and raw materials are booming.

workers complained that the company reneged on its promises to pay an annual 3,000 yuan heating subsidy and health-care and pension benefits.

As the SOEs recovered and expanded, they continued shedding workers and fueling the unrest. The numbers employed were cut in half between 1995 and 2002, although this statistic hides the fact that many profitable SOEs were creating new jobs largely for migrant peasant workers. As coal or steel production expanded, or foreigners invested in new factories, employers all refused to hire the laid-off SOE workers, especially those over 40. This situation has left the Northeast with persistent and severe unemployment problems.

Although Shenyang benefited from additional public works spending, this infusion of funds only created new jobs for peasants working on construction sites. It did not absorb the laid-off SOE workers whose only hope is to start up a small business in the services sector. The tertiary industry, which is more labor intensive, can create five times the employment provided by the secondary industry.

So, is China's strategy now working out? The challenge to create enough jobs remains to be met. Chinese planners said that in 2006 China needed to find jobs for 25 million people in the cities. Of these, 4 million will be school or university graduates joining the job market, 3 million will be peasants moving to the cities, and 13 million are workers let go or about to be retrenched by their employers as a result of the continuous restructuring of SOEs. Economic growth and the natural retirement of workers are expected to create 11 million jobs. This estimate leaves a gap of 14 million. The number of unemployed Chinese in cities is about to hit 17 million in 2006, the peak year as outlined in the 11th five-year economic development plan. The annual average number of jobless people will be 12.3 million during the 2006 to 2010 period.

China's SOEs, like the state factories of East Germany, have proved stubbornly hard to salvage. After absorbing huge subsidies, the debts have continued piling up, and so the party is in the end being forced to let go of its ownership of the state sector. The legacy will linger on for some time. SOE managers have siphoned off so much of the SOE pension funds that it has been difficult to pool enough funds to create a new welfare system to help pensioners.

It is possible that, in the end, one will look back and say all the

Laid-off state workers in Liaoning Province—one man carrying a sign advertising his heavy labor and demolition skills—wait for job offers on the street.

effort to save the SOEs has merely put off the evil day of reckoning. Much of China's heavy industry production remains highly inefficient. It takes, for example, six times more energy and labor to produce steel in China than in any other major steel-producing company. The return on assets remains less than 3 percent and the debts keep accumulating. The Communist Party is increasingly committed to privatizing even the giant SOEs. Sooner or later, it will sell off its stake in the listed SOEs and make them accountable to shareholders. Even the commanding heights of the state economy will be put onto the block.

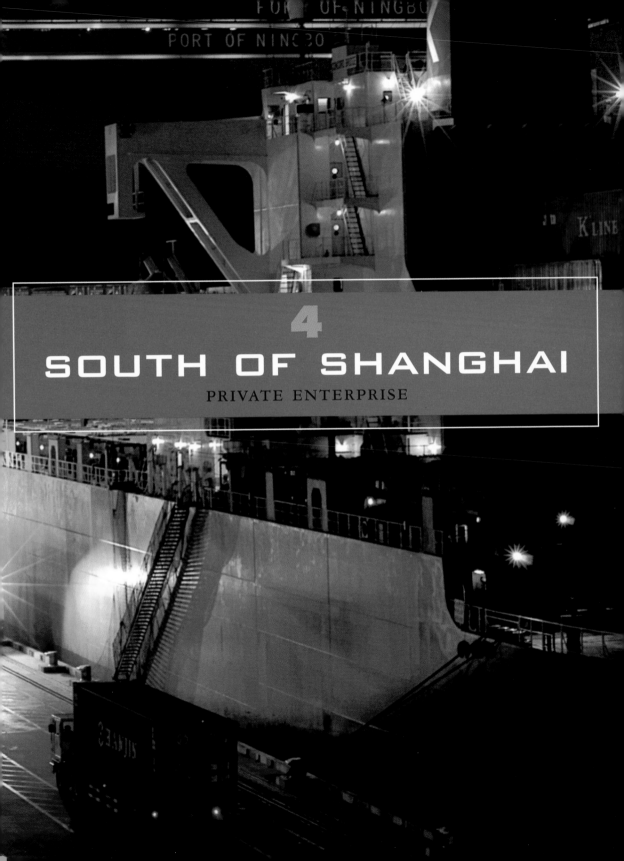

4
SOUTH OF SHANGHAI
PRIVATE ENTERPRISE

CHAPTER FOUR

Unless you normally buy gloves by the million, you will not have heard of Yiting Township or even the neighboring city of Yiwu in Zhejiang Province. It is a small cluster of two- or three-story brick houses set among paddy fields and ponds about two hours' drive south of Hangzhou in eastern China.

The peasants here not only churn out gloves by the billion but also most of the world's socks, ties, zippers, shoes, and hundreds of other small household items. This area is where buyers from Wal-Mart, Sogo, and Woolworth come when they want to stock the shelves of supermarkets on the other side of the world.

Chen Chengsheng, a small, dark-skinned man, was holding a stem of sugarcane in one hand and shouting into a mobile phone held by the other. When I turned up, a buyer from Guangdong was calling. "He wants to know when I can deliver three million of these work gloves to a Japanese buyer," Mr. Chen explained after spitting out some chewed-up cane onto the ground. "It's for a big supermarket and they need it right away." Last year his little factory with 38 workers made ten million gloves, so Mr. Chen thought he could help. The negotiations continued with a series of grunted exclamations. "*Hao, hao!*—Good, good," he concluded and then hung up abruptly.

"I can't make them all, but I can get my neighbors to help out," Mr. Chen explained. In his little village there are seven other factories just like his. I wondered aloud where his factory was, as I hadn't noticed his

Girls like these, dressed in their New Year's finery in their Zhejiang Province village, form the backbone of the workforce in light manufacturing.

PREVIOUS PAGES
Millions of shipping containers— here at Ningbo port—carry the wares of thousands of southern Chinese factories to every imaginable destination around the globe.

or any others when my taxi arrived following the dirt road that ended at Yiting Township. "I'll show you," he said helpfully.

We entered his house by squeezing past a truck that had backed into his front door so that boxes of finished gloves could be loaded into the rear. To the right of the entrance hall was his office, which had a kitchen table, a desk with a computer and a fax machine, and on the wall a grubby calendar with pictures of the god of wealth. On the left-hand side of the entrance hall, we walked straight into his "factory."

It was a front parlor into which he had crammed 14 spinning machines. Each had a spindle with white cotton thread that perched on top and slowly unwound. A white cotton glove dropped every few minutes from the bottom of the machine into a plastic basket. A couple of girls moved about the room, either loading a fresh cotton-thread spindle or removing a full basket of gloves to a neighboring room, actually a brick extension to the house equipped with a large air extractor. Inside, more workers were operating a press that stamped a yellow- or red-colored grip onto the palm of the glove and a steam iron that pressed the gloves before they were packed. Another couple of girls squatted on the stamped-mud ground deftly sorting the gloves, sticking on labels, and then stuffing them into wrappers, before the finished product was tossed into cardboard boxes. And that was it—the gloves were ready for shipment.

Nobody said much as they worked against the steady background hum of the machines that run through the night. Perhaps there was not much talking needed for this sort of work. The workers, all migrant laborers, came from inland provinces like Jiangxi, Hunan, and Henan. Mr. Chen paid them about a hundred dollars a month, and when there was a rush of orders, they worked three shifts a day.

Mr. Chen ran the business with his wife, with whom he had a four-year-old son. He was 32 and had founded the Yiwu Jia Wei Gloves Factory business soon after he left middle school in 1989. At first, they made the gloves by hand at home to supplement their farming income. Then in 1992, they bought some Japanese machinery. Now the machines were all domestically made and several of them, he proudly pointed out, were computerized. "At first it was all domestic sales, but now everything is for export. We export to the United States, South America,

A woman sews suits at the Youngor Group textile factory in Ningbo, Zhejiang Province. Profits are reinvested by Chinese entrepreneurs, leading to bigger factories, newer equipment, and more employees.

Singapore, and Japan," he said. When I asked him if he had ever been abroad himself, he looked faintly astonished at the thought.

Then we sat in the office, drinking green tea out of plastic throw-away beakers, and discussed his business development strategy. Mr. Chen admitted he was now rich, a yuan millionaire. I noticed his wife had splurged on a modish hairstyle, cut short and dyed a fashionable tawny color, but he stressed that he always reinvested profits into expanding production. And that is what everyone did. So output had doubled in the last two years, although profits had been weakened by rising raw material prices. He rarely took out bank loans; if he needed more capital he borrowed from relatives, at a lower interest rate. "Of course, those people who expanded really quickly and did really well had special relations with the government," he said. Some nearby factory owners had grown so fast that they employed 10,000 workers.

Like most people I met in Zhejiang, Mr. Chen left me with the impression that his good fortune had taken him by surprise and that even now he still couldn't quite work out how it all happened or why his business had grown so quickly and so easily. Indeed, it is fair to say that the success of private capitalism in Zhejiang took everyone by surprise. No Western economist nor Communist Party leader had ever predicted that Zhejiang would emerge with the highest concentration of private entrepreneurs in the whole country, or that the province with 47.2 million people would become the richest in China, measured on a per capita basis. How did it all happen?

In 1979 Deng Xiaoping, de facto leader of China, had planned that Guangdong and its fenced-off special economic zones (SEZs) like Shenzhen, Zhuhai, and Shantou would take the lead in China's new economy. Under tightly controlled experimental laboratory conditions, foreign capital would be allowed to employ Chinese labor and power China's export drive. However, an ever larger part of China's 200-billion-dollar-plus trade surplus with the United States is being taken by products made by private businessmen like Mr. Chen. Wal-Mart alone accounts for imports of light industrial goods worth 15 billion dollars a year. China's top leaders, after lifetimes devoted to central planning and Marxism theories, probably could not imagine how much energy they would unleash with the reforms.

The last time I had visited Zhejiang, in 1986, these small privately run factories seemed intriguing but not very impressive. At that time people were just beginning to talk up what was dubbed the "Wenzhou model." In the late 1980s, Wenzhou, a small coastal city and former treaty port with eight million people, was making buttons, jewelry, and all kinds of haberdashery. As the Chinese discarded their drab utilitarian Mao suits, everybody wanted this stuff, which state factories failed to produce in the right quantity or variety. Wenzhou had covered markets with hundreds of stalls, each selling thousands of designs of simple manufactured goods. Other markets offered shoes of every description.

The "Wenzhou model" calls for residents of small manufacturing towns to take goods far afield to customers.

Wenzhou peddlers fanned out all over China, often lugging the goods by hand onto China's overcrowded buses and trains. Soon, little colonies of Wenzhou people were in all the main cities hawking their wares. Often they ran into trouble with the local police. Most people looked down on them as at best unrespectable and at worst semicriminals. But the Wenzhou residents didn't seem to care; they didn't need the state's help, and they were getting rich. (My hosts delighted in treating me to extravagant meals of seafood.)

At the time, the world's button capital was very poorly served by communications. There were no flights or trains, and it took a taxi more than eight hours to drive from Zhejiang's capital, Hangzhou, on roads that traversed mountains and

narrow river valleys. The Communist state had invested little or nothing in Wenzhou. This was a strategic decision because this southern coast faced a possible U.S.-backed invasion from Taiwan. And it was an ideological choice; for centuries, Wenzhou's residents had flaunted the commands of various emperors far away in Beijing by engaging in foreign trade or sometimes piracy. Many had left as bonded laborers and ended up in Hawaii or America. Wenzhou communities can be found in the most unexpected places, like Amsterdam and Paris. Several counties still get into trouble because residents remain heavily involved in smuggling workers into Europe or the United States.

One reason people wanted to leave Wenzhou becomes obvious when you go there. As with much of the southern China coast all the way down to the Pearl River, the population has long outgrown the arable land available. A narrow coastal strip is crowded, and when locals moved into the hills, they cut down the trees and silted up the rivers. Harvests declined, and people had no choice but to look outward to find ways of earning a livelihood through trade. Much the same goes for the Fujianese and the Cantonese, who emigrated in large numbers to Southeast Asia from the 18th century on. There are now an estimated 40 million overseas Chinese, and they form the wealthiest business group in Indonesia, Thailand, Singapore, Malaysia, Vietnam, and several other nations.

Wenzhou's geographical isolation and narrow valleys created an inbred clannish spirit. People from one valley found the language spoken by those in the next valley incomprehensible, and Wenzhou residents were easily suspected of belonging to secret mafia-like triad fraternities, the world's largest criminal society.

When the Chinese Communist Party (CCP) took power in 1949, it mistrusted the people in this part of China. Nationalist leader Chiang Kai-shek's home village is in Zhejiang, and many Zhejiang merchants had been strong supporters of the Nationalists. As Chairman Mao Zedong cut off links with the outside world, anyone with relations abroad or who had a capitalist family background—as many in this region did—automatically went on a blacklist as being politically untrustworthy.

After 1949, Mao's government quickly expropriated the property of both rich and poor in a rush to realize the dream of Marx—the abolition of all private property. The CCP's Chinese name, Gong Chang Dang, literally means "the party of public ownership." By 1959, the possessions of businessmen and peasants had been confiscated, and instead of money, the state created an elaborate rationing system. You needed ration tickets for everything—even hot water.

Wenzhou's residents suffered under this system. There were harsh political campaigns against "capitalists" who secretly tried to dabble in private farming or trade. Mao treated all capitalists and landlords as incurable criminals and continually warned that the "spontaneous forces of capitalism" could reemerge the moment the party's vigilance was dropped. The state forced farmers to grow grain and to cut down their tea bushes and fruit trees. Instead they had to terrace hillsides to create more fields for grain, but still the result was poor harvests and food shortages.

When Deng Xiaoping came to power in 1977, he famously said "to get rich is glorious," but in fact attitudes to the private sector switched back and forth all the time. The party leadership sometimes praised the private sector, sometimes vilified it. Article 12 of China's constitution stated that "publicly owned assets are sacred and public ownership can never be diluted." But when the constitution was revised by reformists in 1988, the new wording carefully avoided introducing the term *private* in favor of the vaguer *individual economy*. This caution was shown even at a time when the reformist wing of the party in charge and the press was trumpeting the contributions of private entrepreneurs. The media boasted with pride that the country had 22 million people considered very rich.

When the party swung to the left, as it did in 1983 and again after 1989, Wenzhou entrepreneurs were singled out in political campaigns and stripped of their wealth. Some were thrown in jail after being accused of evading taxes. After 1989, the party closed a million of the 14.5 million private companies in the country. Following Mao's death in 1976, Wenzhou was perhaps quick off the mark to seize the new opportunities, but its businessmen tried when they could to hide what they were doing. The party only permitted household enterprises to hire a maximum of six workers, but the entrepreneurs would ignore such restrictions. Many resorted to what was called "wearing a red hat." That phrase meant pretending to be a collectively run village or township enterprise, hoping this pretext would protect them from ideological campaigns and screen inspectors.

The term *township* was invented when the people's communes were officially dissolved in 1984. Each commune had had an administrative headquarters from which the lives of thousands of peasants and their families were ordered. Many commune headquarters were established in what had been market towns before 1949. Some of these market towns in the Yangtze Delta, which includes part of Zhejiang Province and Jiangsu Province, had always been extremely prosperous. One reason is that it was easy to transport goods in this region along the network of rivers and canals. Suzhou and Hangzhou on the Grand Canal were the

richest of these towns and were filled with beautiful mansions and gardens. About ten of the lesser towns have recently been restored and turned into tourist attractions where visitors are poled along canals, passing under quaint humpbacked bridges, listening to songs sung by "gondoliers" dressed in traditional garb. Afterward the visitors dine at tables set on flagstone terraces or timbered balconies.

As a Venetian, Marco Polo was not easily impressed, but he found Hangzhou overwhelming. In the 13th century, the city had more than a million residents, ten times as many as his native Venice, which was then the richest trading center in Europe. It would take another five hundred years before any Western city had a population that could rival Hangzhou's.

Marco Polo noted that:

In each of the squares is held a market three days in the week, frequented by 40,000 or 50,000 persons, who bring thither for sale every possible necessary of life. ... All the ten market places are encompassed by lofty houses, and below these are shops where all sorts of crafts are carried on, and all sorts of wares are on sale, including spices and jewels and pearls. Some of these shops are entirely devoted to the sale of wine made from rice and spices, which is constantly made fresh, and is sold very cheap.

When the Communist state outlawed markets, and by extension the sort of services that market towns offer the surrounding district, the population of these market towns fell as people were sent away to work on the land. However, as soon as rural markets reopened after 1979, people quickly moved back into the towns and eagerly opened new businesses. The most dynamic market towns began to specialize in particular products. Hangzhou had a sweater market, Haining a leather market, but the biggest and most successful of all these retail centers emerged in Yiwu, just 30 miles or so from Chen Chengsheng's little factory. The sprawling city of 700,000 was surrounded by an expanding circle of industrial zones, and mile after mile of factories that employed another 700,000 migrant workers. More buildings to house more markets were going up all the time.

I stayed at a brand-new luxury hotel built beside the vast new emporium Yiwu had erected a year or two earlier to replace the old street market. It took an hour to walk from one end of the five-story retail market to the other and the better of a day to explore it. A big banner that hung from ceiling to floor said, "Build the largest market in the world." I wasn't sure whether this was a promise or already a reality.

I stopped at one shop that was staffed by a couple of women from Yongjang Township to look at a display of their products, ranging from Italian espresso pots to wine-cork pullers to motor vehicle brake pads. "We can fulfill any kind of order. Just tell us what you want!" said a cheerful middle-aged woman called Zhu Hualan. She began punching out prices on a large calculator, and I was soon marveling at how low prices for bulk orders could be.

The retail market had 40,000 other shops like hers, mostly run by women representing factories run by one family or one village. They sat

Hangzhou, a wealthy market town even when Marco Polo saw it, has quickly rebounded from Communist disapproval.

there minding babies and knitting or sometimes playing computer games, while the men were at home running the manufacturing. This part of the emporium was devoted to household goods, but others offered bags of every kind, shoes, costume jewelry, handicrafts, clocks, electronic and electrical goods, toys, games, waterproof gear, umbrellas, camping gear, and even motorbikes.

There were traders speaking in Russian, Arabic, Portuguese, French, English, and even Pushtu, often led by some diminutive local girl who served as guide and translator. In one shop I ran into Ismail Khan, dressed in his native hat and gown, who ran a couple of shops in Peshawar close to the Afghan border and had been coming here for seven years, taking the overland route via Ürümqi in Xinjiang Province. "All the world comes here to buy," he said. "Until about 1987 everybody went to Hong Kong or Singapore. Now it is Yiwu."

On the top floor, I come across a purchasing office for Carrefour, the French supermarket giant, next door to the office for the United Nations High Commissioner for Refugees, which procured plastic water carriers, mugs, spoons, pots, and pans.

What Mr. Khan liked about Yiwu was that it was so easy to fill up a shipping container from the huge variety of goods on display. Nowhere else could you choose from so many different suppliers at once and buy in relatively small quantities. "It is so easy to do business here," he said.

While the armada of containers heading across the Pacific gets all the attention, China has also quietly been filling up the bazaars of the Middle East. Yiwu even has its own large mosque serving the hundreds of Arab traders who live in Yiwu year-round. And there are dozens of restaurants, like Al-Aqsa, which served kebabs from hallal meat. Even in Marco Polo's time, he had noted the Arab trading communities in some trading ports.

Cheap as labor might be in Pakistan or Egypt, Mr. Khan thought that nowhere did it cost less than in China. "China has people like the Saudis have oil," he said pithily. Of course, there was more to it than that. There is an entrepreneurial drive here and a government ready to stand aside.

At another outlet selling clocks, including dozens of varieties shaped like a mosque with little minarets, I asked Guo Meilan, another

Buyers from all over the world converge on the vast Yiwu market in Zhejiang to stock store shelves back home.

of those women with fashionably dyed hair, how it all got started here. "We started 15 years ago and we were really poor then. The houses all around were not like you see them now. They were all broken down. We made everything ourselves and went around the country selling the clocks we could carry on our backs. In the first markets, we just sat on the ground and put them out on a blanket," she recalled.

Yiwu officials alone were ready to seize the chance of hosting a large-scale market. Hangzhou and the regional capital of Jinghua rejected the opportunity on the grounds that the markets were too dirty and politically risky. Yiwu kept investing and expanding the marketplace so that this new building was the fourth incarnation of the Yiwu market. Its location lent it a geographical edge over Wenzhou. The city is only a few hours' drive from both Shanghai and

Ningbo, the latter one of the biggest and most favored ports in China, so the goods can be easily shipped abroad.

Despite the modest beginnings of their business, Guo Meilan's husband is now president of the Yiwu City Guanghua Electronics Company (as well as vice chairman of the Yiwu City Clock Association) and employs more than a thousand workers. "We never spent the profits on anything—we kept on expanding—except for the house. You should see it, it is really big with four stories," she said.

Yiwu is more famous for socks than clocks. The nearby town of Dongyang churns out nine billion socks a year, more than enough to warm every pair of feet on the planet. A selection is on display at a separate wholesale market devoted to socks, and that is where I met Zhu Zhixing, president of Dongyang City Good Brother Enterprises. He told me that when Yiwu hosts its regular sock fairs, 100,000 buyers throng through his stalls, but as this was a slow day, he had time to drive me to his factory in Dongyang. We set off in his new Shanghai-made Buick, and along the way we passed a lot of villages with houses all of which he said contained little sock factories. His was a medium-size firm, but Yiwu had a few really big manufacturers like Wen Longjing and his brother who own the Liangsha Company that employs 10,000 workers. They have even opened a subsidiary in the United States to counter the criticism that China is stealing American jobs.

Zhu's family ran three factories, and as we inspected the newest one, I was struck again by just how few workers he employed to turn out these vast quantities of socks, even though textiles is commonly labeled a labor-intensive industry. Most of the workforce was needed for the packaging operation. Things had changed since the first textile factories opened in Lancashire in 18th-century England. Zhu didn't wear a top hat or carry a fob watch, but he was a capitalist even if, like everyone else here, he was still registered as a peasant.

"So how did *you* become such a big capitalist boss?" I teased him when the tour was over. By then we were sitting on traditional heavy wooden furniture in a sparely furnished living room dominated by a TV and stereo system so big they covered most of a wall.

"Well, this is a special kind of socialism we have in China," he laughed, quite unoffended. "Deng Xiaoping called it 'socialism with

Chinese characteristics.' You know, people attribute everything to Deng Xiaoping but people here had secretly started making and selling things like socks even before his reforms, even though it was illegal," he confided.

The big Shanghai factories began outsourcing production in the 1970s, which gave the surrounding areas in the Yangtze Delta a head start when the reforms got under way. Soon the state factories began to face competition and they found it hard to compete. When a state factory wanted to hire new workers, it had to give them jobs for life, housing, pensions, and schools; it could not fire lazy or redundant workers. As this new source of production was illegal, it was put under the rubric "township and village enterprises" so it did not show up in official statistics for a long time.

One Chinese official said the phenomenon was "as if a vast army had suddenly appeared." It meant that the Chinese economy turned out to be much bigger than was recognized. As so often in China, events on the ground ran ahead of the official picture. Before the government took in the changes, Shanghai's state-run factories with their costly cradle-to-grave welfare systems were running into debt. "They were top heavy. For every three workers, there was an administrator and three pensioners to fund. And it always took them a long time to decide anything," Zhu said.

For ideological reasons, the party promoted township and village enterprises that were collectives run by the local party committees. As such, they could easily find investment capital by borrowing from state-run banks and cooperative banks. Local governments wanted to go into business because the revenues from such enterprises were used to pay salaries and perks for their own officials, who splurged on fleets of pricey cars. Even in poor counties, officials commonly drive around in A6 Audis or Toyota Land Cruisers.

Across China, the shortages ended. Instead, there was a vast overinvestment in one sector after another. Overcapacity made competition very stiff. In shoemaking, China had enough factories to make nine billion pairs of shoes a year by the early 1990s, far more than the domestic market could absorb. By the mid-1990s, the country had capacity to make 70 million bicycles a year though the market needed only 30 million. The state manufacturers of famous brands like the Flying Pigeon,

which employed 20,000 workers in Tianjin, went bust.

Zhejiang's capitalists like Zhu didn't have MBAs, or any higher education for that matter. They simply hired cheap labor and responded nimbly to the market. Some 80 percent of private entrepreneurs are ex-farmers and 70 percent have only a middle school education or less. Yet they rapidly triumphed over the collective enterprises run by committees of party officials. Across China, local government administrations piled up huge debts that by 2005 totaled one trillion renminbi (125 billion dollars).

As many of these collective factories went bust, private business-men bought them and turned them around, and this transfer enabled the successful entrepreneur to expand very quickly. For instance, in Yiwu more than half the world's zippers are now made by a handful of companies like Weihai Lalian. Another town nearby, Shenzhou, supplies the world with 90 percent of its neckties.

By the turn of the 21st century, the success of the family-run firms, that is, the Wenzhou model, had created a new class of nouveau riche in China. Now they were faced with an unexpected challenge: What to do with their money?

Zhu told me he was investing all his spare capital in real estate, buying property in Beijing and Shanghai. Real estate agents in these cities all have stories of Wenzhou businessmen marching into their offices with suitcases of money prepared to buy dozens of newly finished apartments in one go. Real estate prices shot up so fast the government feared a bubble was developing.

Other Wenzhou multimillionaires made the news in 2005 when they decided to buy themselves 22 private planes to make getting about the country easier. One man bought himself a Dassault business jet worth 60 million yuan (7.4 million dollars). Tu Changzhong, chairman of the Wenzhou Yikai Group, who snapped up a helicopter, explained why: "It is worthwhile spending millions of yuan on a business jet to save time and energy, and also owning a plane convinces your business partners that you are reliable."

The clout of the newly rich was even felt as far away as New York's auction houses, where Wenzhou millionaires arrived and starting buying all the Chinese antiques that came on the market. One buyer who made a splash became known as "Mr. Pearls," because he had made his fortune by breeding freshwater pearl oysters. Another connoisseur, christened "Mr. Tires," is Lu Hanzhen, president of Kingring Group Company, who by the age of 40 had made a fortune from making motorcycles and the nylon fabric used in tires. He has gained a reputation for paying ten times the listed price to fill out his art collection and even opened a private museum to display to the public some 200 pieces valued at 25 million dollars.

Such ostentatious displays of wealth have spawned a crime wave. Gangs have begun robbing, kidnapping, and murdering rich businessmen at an alarming rate. In February 2002, Zhou Zubao, a Wenzhou fur

Entrepreneurs use new automated systems like this sock machine to produce enormous quantities of clothing.

billionaire, was stabbed to death in front of his mansion. When the murderers were caught and put on trial, *China Daily* reported that Zhou was murdered by some of his business partners over a business deal that went sour. Two received the death sentence and three others, including his nephew, life sentences.[1]

The trial sparked a debate in the press, with some people asking if his death could be attributed to "class hatred." Many of the newly rich have tried to appease public opinion by engaging in ostentatious charity, donating money to the victims of natural disasters or helping widows and orphans. Nan Cunhui, another Wenzhou billionaire, who started making light switches at the age of 21 and later made it onto the Forbes list of the 100 richest people in China, has donated six million dollars for charitable projects. "You'll be respected and esteemed ... when you repay to society ... what you have got with support and nurturing of people at large," Nan told the press.

Getting on the Forbes list has caused the rich other problems. The publicity drew the attention of the leadership. When the list was first published, it prompted then premier Zhu Rongji to ask: "Why is it that the richer the people are, the less tax they pay?" An official survey found that only 4 of China's 50 richest individuals paid any income tax at all. In the ensuing crackdown, the glamorous starlet Liu Xiaoqing was packed off to jail after being accused of evading taxes worth 10 million yuan (1.2 million dollars).

Even more alarming for the party was the discovery that as much as 20 percent of its members were running private companies or semi-privatized state factories and were wealthy enough to be considered capitalists. After great debate, the party announced in 1987 that it would accept private businessmen into its ranks. A star delegate to the 1987 party congress was Mrs. Guang Guangmei, a party official in the coal-and-steel town of Benxi, Liaoning Province, who had leased eight bankrupt state shops and within two years turned them around, earning more than 44,000 yuan in profits.

Many like Guang found themselves ejected from the same party a year later in 1989 after the Tiananmen massacre. Some private businessmen had actively supported the student demands for democracy, and one prominent businessman had used his computer company to support an influential think tank. Later, the then party leader Jiang Zemin declared that in the future no more businessmen would be allowed into the party. Ten years down the road, when the party celebrated its 80th anniversary, Jiang had to lift the ban. The first businessman to be formally inducted was none other than Nan Cunhui, the Wenzhou tycoon and public benefactor.

The party had no choice but to change tack. As the downsizing of the state bureaucracy and state-owned enterprises got under way, the party actively encouraged officials to "jump into the sea" of commerce, or *xia hai,* as the only alternative to *xia gang,* meaning "to step down from their posts" and be made redundant. Every ministry, even the Ministry of Foreign Affairs, had to create business, partly to earn money and partly to deploy redundant workers. The People's Liberation Army was no exception and ended up creating a commercial empire that even used navy vessels to smuggle in everything from cars to petrol.

Naturally, all this shift toward commerce spawned a murky sea of official corruption that stirred up public anger against the party. Officials, especially the children of powerful bureaucrats, set up "briefcase companies." They could use their connections, their *guangxi,* to obtain goods and services in short supply, buy them at state-fixed prices, and then sell them for a big markup on the free market. To have a dual pricing system in an economy of shortages (like China's in the 1980s) was to license profiteering on a huge scale; this corruption was given the name *guandao.* Everyone's children, from those of Deng Xiaoping downward, became entangled in these "economic crimes." The reformers tried to counter public indignation by first arresting and then even executing some of these "princelings." This action so enraged powerful and conservative party veterans who found themselves unable to protect their offspring that they turned against the reformers, like Party Secretary Hu Yaobang, and pushed them out of office.

In the early 1990s, China phased out the dual pricing system. By 2000, the market determined the prices for 90 percent of products, although the state still controlled key sectors such as energy and grain. Shortages of many products disappeared, and China became more concerned about deflation rather than inflation. The new wave of economic reforms, especially the creation of a real estate market and financial mar-

kets, however, created fresh opportunities for official corruption. Those with the right guangxi could easily obtain land cheaply, or simply expropriate it from hapless peasants, and sell leases to real estate developers.

When state companies began to list on exchanges at home and abroad, the princelings found fresh opportunities for enrichment, selling off state assets that were supposed to be in public ownership. Mostly big enterprises were listed; smaller and medium-size enterprises were disposed of in a less public manner. Local officials or their relatives engaged in asset stripping: The profitable parts of an enterprise were sold off in a murky fashion, leaving the indebted or unproductive part on the books of the state banks. Debt was public but profit was private.

The debts and pension liabilities of many failed enterprises quickly mounted up. The party was reluctant to allow such "zombie companies" to officially go bankrupt. One key reason was the absence of a national social welfare system to pay the subsistence wages to the unemployed, pensions of retirees, and housing and health-care costs of former state employees.

The cumulative result of all these trends left the distinction between the private and public sectors, and between businessmen and officials, hopelessly blurred. Neither Adam Smith nor Karl Marx ever contemplated such a situation when they developed their theories on how states operate. The confusion was compounded by the fact that in China there is also no real distinction between the bureaucracy and the Communist Party. With only a few exceptions, any civil servant of any importance is simultaneously a party member, and hence a member of a separate and secretive organization. This melding of party and government was another consequence of the Tiananmen massacre. The reformist wing of the party had stood in favor of a separation of the two, but after 1989 the issue was shelved.

When, 15 years after Tiananmen, economists at the OECD (Organization for Economic Cooperation and Development) in Paris set about trying to calculate the size of the private sector in China, they found it difficult to sort through Chinese statistics and their outdated definitions. They did come up with the following, and somewhat astonishing, conclusion, however: The private sector now accounted for two-thirds of the economy. Hitherto, Chinese statistics had indicated that the private sector, excluding foreign-controlled firms, accounted for about one-third of gross domestic product. In other words, China was now said to be operating more of a market economy than Britain or Germany, where the state accounts for around 44 percent of GDP.

The OECD report also concluded that the change involved more than juggling definitions: "About one-third of the increase in the private sector share is mirrored in a decline in the number and output of collectives, with the remaining two-thirds reflected in closure and divestment of solely state-owned firms." From 1998 onward, private businessmen had taken over more and more collective and state firms.[2]

By 2003, there were officially 3 million domestic private enterprises and 24 million sole proprietorships (*getihu* enterprises) registered, but it was clear that many enterprises, especially in the service sectors, were not registered. So the size of the private sector, and the economy as a whole, was probably understated.

Private-sector industrial employment almost tripled between 1998 and 2004, which showed that the private sector was best at creating most

Small workshops throughout Yongkang County use punch-presses to produce various metal parts, like the bicycle pump parts being made here.

of the 18 million new jobs China needs to create every year. These private companies each had an average of 18 employees; fewer than 5 percent had more than 500 employees. One survey quoted by the OECD report said that the private firms grew by 23 percent a year on average, with one in ten firms doubling in size every two years. By contrast, employment in state-controlled industrial companies fell by almost 40 percent from 1998 to 2003, as 16 million workers were laid off.

The private sector, especially the successful firms found in Zhejiang, is concentrated along the eastern seaboard and in a handful of big cities. This trend created an alarming regional disparity as the inland provinces, many with huge populations of 60 million or more, remained mired in poverty. The OECD report observed: "An overwhelming share of private industrial output is produced in the eastern coastal region (especially Zhejiang, Guangdong and Jiangsu Provinces) that has been at the forefront of all types of reforms. In this region, the share of industrial value added from the private sector is 63% against only 32% in other regions."

In Chairman Mao's time, the party pursued egalitarianism and policies intended to spread the benefits of development equitably across the whole country. In practice, the economic planners concentrated investment in the Northeast and the interior of the country, sometimes for strategic reasons. Deng Xiaoping's reforms reversed that trend under the rubric of "allowing some people to get rich first."

By 1987, this approach was further elaborated into the "Gold Coast strategy" of encouraging investment in the coastal provinces. As the regional gap widened, the state responded by pumping investment into large projects in the poorer and western regions. Yet after 2000, it became ever clear that if the private sector was best at creating jobs, then the solution was to further encourage the privatization of the economies of the inland provinces and the interior. To help them, then, the best thing the state could do was to get involved less, not more.

When Chinese economists published such calls, one had to ask what the long-term implications are. Chinese leaders are fond of coining and employing phrases like Deng's—"It does not matter if a cat is black or white, as long as it catches mice." Yet it clearly must matter, when the ruling party is called the Party of Public Property but an

Two lab technicians inspect the quality of mobile phone handsets at the Ninbo Bird factory in Fenghua, Zhejiang Province. Stiff competition from both domestic and foreign brands in an already saturated market has prompted the company to start its own R&D center and seek markets abroad.

ever growing number of its members are either capitalists or officials who favor private property. Will the party one day rename itself the Party of Private Property?

The success of Zhejiang's Wenzhou model, really another term for laissez-faire economics, could not have taken place without government intervention of various kinds. It required local officials to foster the right environment for growth. In places like Yiwu, the authorities quickly cleared farmland to build industrial zones and invested in new buildings like the retail mall. They built roads and ports and power stations at a remarkable rate, often without the lengthy planning procedures and consultations that are common elsewhere. Without this government-backed infrastructure, business could not flourish.

Perhaps the most remarkable impetus to development has been the telecommunications revolution in China, especially the ready embrace of mobile phone technology. In 1986, the whole country was served with fewer than 2,000 international telephone and telex lines. In major cities, only officials had phone lines and there was one phone line for every 159 people. The country now has more than 300 million mobile phone users, more than the United States. Between 1998 and 2004, the annual average growth rate of China's mobile phone market was 84.9 percent, three times faster than the fixed-line phone market.

The speed at which the state has built new roads has been equally remarkable. In ten years, the country constructed a highway system as big as Germany's and built many minor roads linking small towns and villages. The combination of instant mobile phone communications and a modern road system has created a unique environment: a First World infrastructure with Third World wages.

The capital market has also developed in ways that defy conventional wisdom. By 2005, China had private savings of at least 12 trillion yuan (1.4 trillion dollars) sitting in the banks. People saved because, in the absence of a welfare state, they feared for their future and worried about how to pay for emergencies like medical bills, but most of the savings remained idle in state banks. The Zhejiang private economy has grown despite the bank savings.

Wenzhou was the first place in the country to operate private banks, and most of its entrepreneurs raise capital outside the state banking system. As most businesses retain such a large share of their profits, they therefore often do not need to obtain the backing of the local or central government to finance expansion. In any case, the private sector could not draw loans from state-owned banks or raise capital on the stock markets because the financial system is designed to help state or collective enterprises.

The private enterprises, therefore, flourish largely independent of the state and free of many of the restrictions seen in heavily regulated Western economies. Factories in Yiwu have profited from the most unregulated labor market in the world. The cost of labor is set entirely by the market without government supervision. Workers switch jobs the moment they discover another factory down the road offers slightly higher wages. Employers have no need to be responsible for providing any welfare benefits or security and hire and fire workers at will.

The human toll, including deaths and injuries from industrial accidents, is very high and is described in the next chapter. The cost in terms of environmental damage is very high, too. "Pollution is a time bomb for the Yangtze River Delta," warned one writer in the *China Daily.* "It has to be defused before it is too late. The country cannot afford for one of its most prosperous and most densely populated regions to become unsuitable for human habitation."[3] The article described the case of Zhejiang's Changxing County, whose 175 factories produce 65 percent of all China's car batteries. So much industrial waste was discharged into the river that it killed off the fish and shrimp and made local agricultural staples— rice, tea, peaches, and plums—both inedible and unsaleable.

Where does the Wenzhou model go from here? Is such rapid growth sustainable? Or will it succumb to competition by start-ups in other parts of China or other low-cost countries like India? In Yiwu, I visited one of the larger businesses, the Neoglory Jewelry Company, to see how it was developing. Neoglory makes fashion jewelry in the Qingkou industrial zone, which employs 5,000 workers. Like all the others, it is very much a family-run business, founded by Mrs. Zhou Shaoguang, who started out at the age of 18 in 1978. The eldest in a poor family with six children, she started out making jewelry at home and selling her wares around the country from a basket. By 1988, she had saved enough to open her first stall at the Yiwu market but still had no

employees. Then in 1990 she went to Europe by herself to visit the Paris jewelry trade fair and, inspired by what she saw there, she came back and started making imitations of the Parisian designs.

The new products began to sell well and the Yiwu area, like Wenzhou itself, became a center for making costume jewelry, buttons, and haberdashery. Within a few years, she had opened a factory with 300 workers and then kept expanding. In 1998, she persuaded the Yiwu government to give her a loan of one million yuan and by 2004 entered the fourth stage of expansion. The large showroom displayed literally thousands of different product lines, and the company was exporting goods worth ten million dollars. The biggest market was in the United States, but more than 70 percent of the products were still sold in China.

Like the Zhejiang private businesses, the company had grown by relying on copies or imitations of foreign designs and introducing them to the huge and still untapped domestic market. In this sector, there were no state factories to compete with, and unlike many foreign investors, the company could make products cheaply enough to be affordable to the mass-consumer market. In the 1980s, the biggest factories were in Hong Kong. Its biggest tycoon, Li Ka-shing, had started out by making plastic flowers, using cheap refugee labor in the 1960s. Such factories had moved across the border into Guangdong after 1980, and many Yiwu companies got their start by buying machinery and getting designs and orders from Guangdong.

The hub of the industry remains the Canton Fair and the top-quality products are still made in Guangdong, but Yiwu is rapidly catching up. It is fast becoming a rival cluster, with thousands of other factories and hundreds of wholesale outlets spread around the city. Yiwu companies are now in position to cut out the Hong Kong middleman and sell directly abroad. Zhou Shaoguang is also doing what the Hong Kong businessmen failed to do: Her company has set up a chain of retail outlets across China. When I visited, Neoglory already operated 12 shops and had opened its first overseas shop in Dubai. It had also formed a partnership with Swarovski, a big upscale European brand. The family had, like Li Ka-shing before them, diversified into property. Mrs. Zhou's husband, Yu Wenxin, was buying up properties in Shanghai.

Like all the others in Zhejiang, Neoglory remains very much a family-run enterprise. All 30 of them—sisters, husbands, and children—occupy the fifth and sixth floors of the factory. Many of them are involved in business. The third sister works in Hong Kong while the fourth sister is studying in Australia. Mrs. Zhou's eldest son is at school in England.

It is too early to say whether such peasant entrepreneurs will be able to continue their success and master the next stage by going on to create a successful company or an international brand. In 2005, the Zhejiang government became sufficiently concerned about this question that it decided to send, at public expense, 30 such tycoons to take part in a 12-day special training course in business. So far only a handful of China's private enterprises have made it onto the list of China's biggest 500 companies and few of them have created a domestic brand, let alone a global one. Much depends on the next generation, who, should they wish to study management at Tsinghua University in Beijing, will be better educated and qualified to develop family businesses.

How the Communist Party will adjust to the reality of the growing role of the private sector is another unknown. In 1998, China amended the constitution to fully recognize private ownership and private enterprise, while insisting that state ownership would remain the dominant form of ownership. The amendment states that "individual, private and other non-public economies are major components of the socialist market economy, and the State protects the lawful rights and interests of individual and private economies." Since then, private companies have been allowed to enter new fields and invest in banking, telecommunications, air travel, utilities, health, education, defense, and oil exploration, distribution, and trade. They are increas-

Luxury knockoffs sold throughout China are popular among consumers, but the perpetuation of copying products rather than creating new ones will not sustain the momentum of economic growth.

ingly being allowed to obtain credit from state banks and raise capital on the stock market.

The private sector is becoming the dominant force in the economy even though the official labels remain in place. China still fights defining itself as a capitalist state. Under the terms of its accession to the World Trade Organization, it will not officially become a market economy before 2014. Yet, as the OECD figures and so much else make clear, events have already overtaken this timetable.

Chinese society has already changed, even though the political system has yet to adapt to the new social order. The vast majority of Chinese are peasants who still lack any legal title to the land they farm and whose incomes have been stagnant for the past 20 years. They provide the 120 million or so migrant workers who flock to the factories in eastern and southern China or who labor in the service sectors of big cities.

In the cities and older industrial areas of China are the workers and their families, a sector of about 100 million. Tens of millions of them have lost their jobs and are now competing with the migrant workers for work. Some have managed to open shops and restaurants in the private sector, but others remain trapped in the old socialist system, dependent on the state. In addition, another 50 million or so work for the state as teachers, doctors and nurses, low-ranking bureaucrats, soldiers, and police on relatively low but stable wages.

Above all, the nouveau-riche class of factory owners, many of them former peasants themselves, are now entering the ranks of the Communist Party. Beyond them are former officials who parlayed their political power into wealth and now own land and enterprises. Just how many belong to these two groups is hard to say, but China probably has a class of wealthy consumers numbering between 100 million and 200 million. This is a group with a purchasing power equal to well-off groups in Japan, Europe, and the United States.

The impact is already being felt across the world. Chinese consumers now account for 11 percent of worldwide revenues of luxury-good brands, and by 2014 one study claims they could be buying 24 percent of all luxury goods.[4] China, for example, was by 2005 BMW's biggest market after Germany for its most luxurious line of cars. The

In southern China, at least, the next generation of entrepreneurs is growing up relatively Westernized and affluent. These young models wait backstage for their appearance in a beauty contest.

World Tourism Organization expects that by 2020 there will be more than 100 million outward-bound Chinese tourists, making China the fourth largest source of international travelers. Chinese tourism expenditure may hit 30 billion dollars by 2008. Chinese students studying overseas are already the largest group of foreign students in universities in Britain and the United States.

All this wealth has been created on the back of an army of low-paid and docile peasant labor. As the next chapter explains, many of them are becoming increasingly angry and frustrated by the social injustice in a society that was once so fanatically committed to achieving absolute egalitarianism.

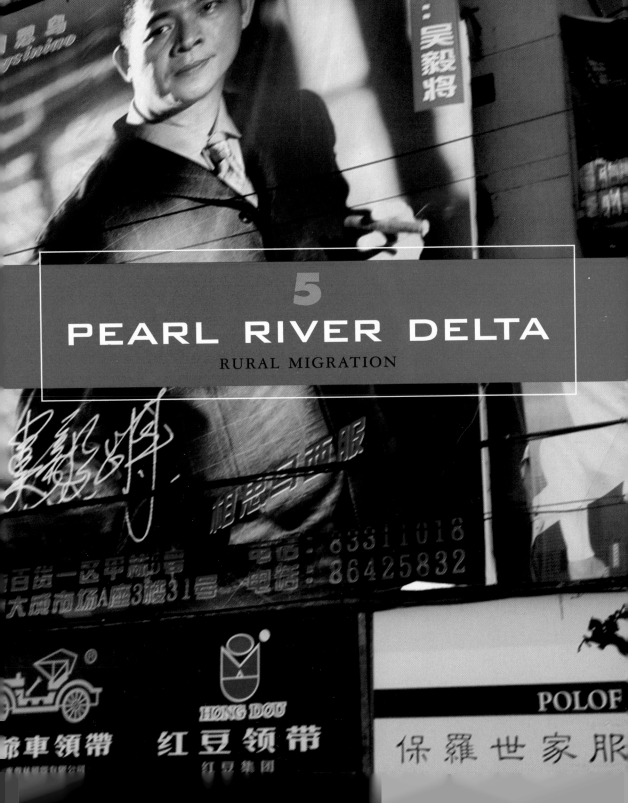

5

PEARL RIVER DELTA

RURAL MIGRATION

CHAPTER FIVE

At seven o'clock on Saturday evening, the girls at the New Science Factory in Dongguan get off their 12-hour shift and stumble wearily toward their dormitory. There are thousands of girls milling around or getting off darkened buses that have arrived from another factory owned by the same electronics firm, but it is oddly quiet.

The girls show their laminated ID cards to the guard, file past a notice board with neat lists of regulations, and trudge up one of the staircases. Each dorm block has eight floors and along each stretches a row of cell-like rooms with a barred window hidden by lines of hanging wash.

Some of the girls soon start coming back down the stairs, then along the street, carrying buckets and dirty clothes to the bathhouse. They file back ready for sleep on a narrow, six-tiered bunk wearing long cotton pajamas. It makes them look innocent, more like children than workers, as if this were a girl's boarding school that had somehow moved into a penitentiary.

Outside the bathhouse, a plump and spotty teenager notices me and wants to start practicing her faltering English. She introduces herself as Zhang Huali from Hunan Province. "Look at their tired faces, as long as a noodle," she says before we switch to Chinese so we can chat more easily about her life.

Like the others, she has just spent 12 hours soldering circuit boards. Miss Zhang looks blank when I ask her what exactly it is she is

Charles Dickens would have recognized today's Chinese factories—like this bike plant in Longhua—as modern versions of Victorian sweatshops.

PREVIOUS PAGES
Migrant workers, like this porter, are mostly impoverished rural peasants who come to urban centers looking for jobs.

making. It is boring, exhausting, repetitive work that dulls the brain. Some girls when they arrive fresh from the countryside have to leave after just a few days. "They just can't stand it," she says, dropping her voice a little and then opening her eyes wide to register surprise: "And some are still doing this after ten years."

"It is hard to get used to the shifts," she says with a yawn. They spend two weeks on the night shift and two weeks on the day shift. "If your dorm is near the road, then the noise makes it difficult to sleep." Miss Zhang has already done two years and is desperate to escape. "I wanted to stay on at school and study English, but my parents had no money for that," she explains wistfully. "We just have a couple of hours off after work, so I try to use it to learn English."

Mastering English, she believes with the inborn optimism of a 20-year-old, will be her passport to a white-collar job and new life in the cities. If she fails, she will return to her parents' village in Hunan, an agricultural province in central China, and marry a boy chosen by her family. Her life will then resemble that of her parents who eke out a subsistence living growing wheat and rice. When the harvest is good, they sell the extra to earn some cash.

Miss Zhang is one of the 36 million peasant girls on whose slight shoulders China's export miracle depends. Without this docile army willing to toil through the night, there would be no fleets of giant ships stacked high with containers crammed with toys, shoes, clothes, and electrical and electronic goods stamped "Made in China."

Like Spanish treasure galleons before them, taking back the gold and silver mined in the New World, the trade seems one way. The ultralarge container ships usually return almost empty across the Pacific. China is accumulating an overflowing treasury. By 2006, China had amassed the world's largest foreign exchange reserves—close to a trillion dollars—by running huge and still growing trade deficits.

It seems to have happened in the blink of an eye. China has gone from being an autarkic isolated recluse to the world's third largest trading nation in just 25 years. Foreign investors from Hong Kong moved the first export-processing factories to a corner of southern Guangdong Province in 1980, but the trickle that turned into a flood after 1992 only really became noticeable after 1998.

China's economic miracle depends on girls from the countryside who leave home to work in the factories.

By 2005, export-processing factories in Guangdong Province alone employed 20 million workers, a population the size of Australia's. On paper, China can claim to have overtaken the United States as the world's largest manufacturer of high-tech electronics goods like computers and mobile phones. Yet while the phenomenon is important, it does not always seem to be quite the evidence of successful modernization it seems to be.

It all rests on the back of what used to be known as "coolie" labor.

It's a word that entered the English dictionary from the Chinese phrase *ku li,* meaning "bitter labor" (or "bitter strength"), when, at the height of 19th-century globalization, Chinese laborers were indentured to work abroad. Some cut cane in Hawaii or built railroads in California, but many worked in the British Empire, growing rice in Burma (present-day Myanmar) or harvesting rubber in Malaya.

This time the work has come to China, rather than the other way around. Consumers around the world everywhere are benefiting from cheaper goods made in China, and profits are enriching the Chinese state in a way that no one in China quite foresaw when it started. Few predicted that out of its tentative beginning China would go on to become the world's emporium. In 1979 Deng Xiaoping opened the first four special economic zones (SEZs) in the hopes of attracting new and modern technology. Three of them, including Shenzhen, are here in Guangdong Province (better known in English as Canton). Dongguan itself has one of the highest concentrations of foreign-invested factories.

This city of 1.5 million, plus hundreds of thousands of overseas Chinese and some 5 million migrant workers, has become the workshop of the world. It plays host to some 18,000 enterprises concentrated here. The biggest factories, like shoe factories, employ 10,000 workers; some employ as many as 40,000.

Half of China's exports are made in Guangdong, and two-thirds of China's exports are now made by foreign-invested firms. The foreign investment keeps rolling in at an annual rate of 50 or 60 billion dollars a year, but the degree of technology transfer taking place is uncertain. The goods are not so much "made" here as assembled here. One soon discovers that in any Chinese factory, the most important and sophisticated part of any product—the sole of the running shoes, the integrated circuits and software in mobile phones, even the compressors in refrigerators—are made and designed elsewhere. While Zhang Huali may be making high-tech goods in her factory, the conditions belong more to the 19th than the 21st century. The workforce employed here is drawn from the most unskilled and uneducated part of China's population.

To the visitor, Dongguan offers a contradictory jumble of impressions. New highways, big shopping malls, and settlements of Western villas surrounded by guards and neatly landscaped flowerbeds and bordered by golf courses with shimmering green grass tell one story. The factories spread out like vast military encampments tell another. Here squads of workers are drilled and marched to and fro wearing the uniforms of global brands such as IBM, Siemens, Nokia, Duracell, and Sanyo. Their barracks, each marked out by a telltale curtain of multicolored washing hanging out to dry, are everywhere.

The speed at which more villas, factories, and highways appear out of the rice fields is astonishing. The building never seems to stop. Everywhere are new half-finished construction sites being scooped out of the red earth.

It all started in 1980 when Deng Xiaoping appealed to overseas Chinese, the "children of the Yellow Emperor," to invest in factories and profit from the low taxes and cheap labor. Hong Kong manufacturers responded, and a new modern city just across the border sprang up in Shenzhen, the first new city built in China in well over 50 years.

Mind-numbing assembly lines working 12-hour days churn out consumer products for the world—these workers are putting together electronic parts at a factory in Panyu, Guangdong Province.

Deng deliberately set about copying the "Hong Kong model." The British followed a laissez-faire pro-business policy in Hong Kong. The colonial government avoided trying to plan the economy and kept income and business taxes very low. The welfare system was minimal, but the government invested in the world's largest government-housing program. Free-market economist Milton Friedman often hailed it as an example of the benefits a free economy could bring. Shenzhen copied Hong Kong's practice of raising revenues by selling off land leases and also kept taxes to 15 percent.

Hong Kong grew as a city of immigrants, as did Shenzhen. Many were refugees who arrived in the colony after 1949. At one end of the social scale were the wealthy Shanghainese. They brought to Hong Kong capital, know-how, and connections, and they built factories and ran shipping companies. At the other end, millions of poor and grateful migrants came, largely from Guangdong, ready to work hard in their new home.

In between the two, the British ran an efficient, honest, colonial administration. Businessmen benefited from a first-class port, a solid British-style legal system, and a stock market. As the only free corner of the Chinese world, it attracted businessmen from all over the Chinese diaspora in Southeast Asia. When mainland China was closed, Taiwan, a dictatorship, was threatened by invasion, and Vietnam and Korea were engulfed by war, everyone came to Hong Kong to conduct their business. Even the Chinese Communist Party chose Hong Kong for its trade and financial transactions with the outside world.

Indeed, Hong Kong survived and flourished despite, and perhaps because of, the wars in Korea and Vietnam and the turmoil of the Cultural Revolution. It rode out the boom and bust of the 1970s oil crisis. After Chairman Mao Zedong's death, it emerged in the 1980s as China's "window on the world." When manufacturing moved across the border, Hong Kong called itself the "shop window," and Shenzhen the "workshop in the backroom."

There was no directly elected government in Hong Kong, although it had a lively civic society and a free press. Instead, the British ran things advised by a council largely drawn from the business and professional elite. Hong Kong Island had been ceded "in perpetuity" by the

Thanks to the great wealth generated by its special economic zone, Shenzhen is one of China's most dynamic cities.

Qing dynasty but a 99-year lease for the larger tract of land on the mainland, the New Territories, ran out in 1997. In the run-up to the handover, Hong Kong's political fate hung in the balance.

Deng Xiaoping's plan to incorporate Hong Kong, Macau, and Taiwan and to legitimize rule over Tibet depended on preventing any kind of plebiscite from taking place. The legitimacy of the claims of the People's Republic rested on the history of military expansion by the Manchus, not on any popular mandate. While elsewhere in the world the government of former colonies came to power after some kind of popular vote, China insisted that Hong Kong should not officially be recognized as a colony. It did not want the British to allow Hong Kong residents to be consulted in a vote or to choose their own leaders.

In the wake of the 1989 Tiananmen massacre, more than one million people in Hong Kong took to the streets, backing demands for democracy not only in China but also in Hong Kong. These demonstrations alarmed the Communist Party and encouraged a new governor, Christopher Patten, a senior Conservative Party politician, to attempt to widen the democratic franchise.

During the acrimonious squabbles over democracy between Beijing and Hong Kong, and Beijing and London, Beijing drew up a basic law for Hong Kong that included a vague timetable for direct elections. However, Beijing continues to block popular demands for reforms that would allow the population to choose its own leaders.

Shenzhen started out as a fenced-off experiment where mainland Chinese needed a special pass to enter (and they still do). For some time, leaders considered using it as a laboratory for political experiments in democracy, but this idea was shelved after 1990. One could say that Hong Kong showed China that a successful economy could in fact be run without democracy. In 1991 Deng Xiaoping urged the Chinese to "create more Hong Kongs," and the Shenzhen SEZ spawned thousands of imitators. At least 2,000 special economic zones opened up in the early 1990s. The largest was Pudong in Shanghai. Eventually there were 10,000 more covering an area of over 6,000 square miles.

Many of these SEZs are really new industrial zones built outside existing urban areas. They house local village and collective enterprises or former "third line" military factories relocated from the remote areas where they had been originally built to hide them from bombing. Yet they all offer investors new infrastructure, tax holidays, low taxes, and cheap union-free peasant labor.

In the SEZs foreign investors enjoy special privileges such as paying only 15 percent tax, compared to the 33 percent tax that state factories had to pay. This tax break has encouraged many Chinese companies to register in Hong Kong or elsewhere and to return as "foreign investors." Hong Kong accounts for two-thirds of all foreign investment, with the next biggest area of investors from the tiny British Virgin Islands. By 2004, China reported that actual direct foreign investment totaled an accumulated 562 billion dollars, of which 190 billion dollars came from Hong Kong and 57 billion dollars from the Virgin Islands.

Hong Kong residents, here marching in a prodemocracy rally in 2004 to mark the seventh anniversary of transfer of power from England to China, have provided much of the capital for Guangdong enterprises.

In 1990 China was exporting goods worth a modest 62 billion dollars, but ten years later the figure was 250 billion dollars, and five years after that, it was shipping out 561 billion dollars' worth of goods. Large waves of foreign investment only began to flow in after 1993 and escalated rapidly in the late 1990s until the level reached a new annual record of 60 billion dollars in 2004.

Such exponential growth has never happened before in history, at least not on this scale nor at this speed. Chinese exports have grown so fast that they seem to overwhelm one industry after another. China now accounts for 60 percent of global trade in textiles, 70 percent of the trade in toys. Even the British Empire at its peak never dominated the world marketplace like this. British textile factories employed less than half a million workers; China's industry employs 19 million people.

Chinese apparel exports doubled in five years to reach 116 billion dollars. Trade has been boosted by recent events. China entered the World Trade Organization (WTO) in 2001 and lifted domestic export-licensing restrictions, while the 30-year-old global trade agreements that allocated export quota amounts to textile-producing countries expired in 2004.

This is not the first time in history that Chinese exports have played a significant role. The ancient silk route, along which Chinese exports flowed, was so lucrative that nomadic tribes in Central Asia, like the Huns and later the Mongols, vied among themselves to control the trade routes. With the resulting wealth, they went on to create great empires. Later European explorers were motivated to circumnavigate the world in an effort to secure this trade by trying to find a direct sea route to China.

In modern times, European nations competed to open trading relations with the Qing dynasty. They wanted to import silk, lacquerware, tea, and porcelain to supply a European craze for Chinoiserie. The emperors in Beijing initially restricted the trade to Canton. After the Opium Wars, China agreed to open the "treaty ports" along the coast, and this created the prosperity of ports like Shanghai and Hong Kong.

Americans are becoming alarmed by their growing trade deficit with China, which reached 200 billion dollars in 2005. China has kept the surplus and accumulated a large portion of U.S. external debts in the form of treasury bonds. Economists warn that U.S. consumer borrowing and U.S. government overspending are being financed by China and that this imbalance cannot continue indefinitely without a major correction.

Western trading nations have become alarmed by trade deficits with China in the past, as well. It was the failure of European nations like Britain to find any goods that the Chinese wanted to buy that led the British to start exporting opium to China. By a quirk of history, it was at Humen, a few miles from Dongguan, where in 1838 the Chinese confiscated and burned the opium. This act triggered the First Opium War—as a result of which China ceded Hong Kong in the first place.

Britain in 1838 was in the midst of the Industrial Revolution, and now the tables have turned. Britain began industrializing after the 1750s and its factories produced low-cost textiles made from local wool or from cotton imported from America. The British searched for foreign markets to sell their surplus. The first governor of Hong Kong, Sir Henry Pottinger, promised that China was an opportunity so great that "all the mills of Lancashire could not make stocking-stuff sufficient for one of its provinces." Now the Lancashire mills are museums and all the textile factories are in Dongguan.

It has led some to compare China with the first industrial revolution in Britain. China's industrial revolution, like Britain's before it, is powered by coal and manned by unskilled peasants driven off the land by advances in agriculture. More than 100 million peasants have left the land. Roughly a third are peasant girls under 28 working in the export-processing factories, another third are their brothers working in mines and construction sites. The rest have moved to urban China to take jobs in the service sector.

The harsh working conditions in Dongguan factories are often described as Dickensian and excused as an inevitable part of the process that Western nations all passed through on their way to becoming wealthy and democratic. The factories don't look like the "dark satanic mills" evoked by the 19th-century English poet William Blake, but factory conditions in China are as harsh, if not harsher, than those 200 years ago.

In the Lancashire mills, women and children worked ten-hour shifts and had Sundays off. In Dongguan, girls like Zhang Huali tend the factory machines working 12-hour shifts with 50 minutes off at lunch and often work seven-day weeks. Most of the jobs are piecework, with wages starting at around 450 yuan a month. The girls are not as young as the children employed in early 19th-century Britain, but many are only 16.

As in Britain, factory work has torn apart families. Miss Zhang has a brother and sister working somewhere in Dongguan, but is not in regular contact with them. She has no time to travel to see them and the family is reunited only at Spring Festival. When I met her, some workers were lining up to get on a bus back home to Hunan. This annual migration, the largest in the world, bears witness to the strength of family ties in China because traveling is so hard. Some factories hire special buses for their workers, but most stand in line for long hours to buy tickets and then travel in crowded trains where there is no room to sit or even to reach the toilets. Some passengers can't handle the poor conditions and jump off the train cars. Others prepare themselves by buying adult diapers.

For Miss Zhang, though, the stresses of her life have proven too great. "I am not going back this year," she announced firmly. "I've broken off ties with my parents." Why, she wouldn't say, but like all the others, she lives a constrictive nun-like existence in these dormitory blocks. Inside, a prison-like discipline reigns. Some factories even stipulate how the girls should place their toothbrushes in their rinse cups and where their face towels should hang. Before work each morning, the girls line up in squads for mandatory gymnastic exercises and are then marched to their work stations by guards. Many Taiwanese factories hire former non-commissioned officers to hone the correct discipline. Any girl who loses her badge or spends too long on a toilet break is punished by a fine. At the factories, there are common rooms to read, watch TV, play Ping-Pong, but there is no time for boyfriends or parties.

When writing *Das Kapital,* Karl Marx based his theories and prophecies of class warfare on his study of British capitalism. It was clear not only to Marx but also to others that capitalism and imperialism brought a twofold misery: first to the new working class and then to those in the colonies like India. Tens of thousands of Indian clothmakers lost their jobs when they couldn't compete with the flood of cheap-

er textiles from Britain. "The misery hardly finds parallel in the history of commerce," India's governor-general, William Bentinck, wrote to his superiors in London in 1834.

Deng Xiaoping's Marxist critics, like the ideologue Hu Qiaomu, said that the SEZs were no better than foreign colonies and accused Deng of selling out the country to foreign capitalists. The Chinese Communist Party rose to power, after all, by helping to organize and lead the workers' protests in Hong Kong, Canton, and Shanghai against wages and conditions in factories that were, indeed, often owned by foreign capitalists. Around the base of the Monument to the People's Heroes in Tiananmen Square is a frieze that celebrates the workers' struggles to establish free-trade unions and gain better working conditions.

The trade unionists in Britain's industrial revolution were pioneers, so it took decades of protest to introduce social reforms that since have become accepted international norms. Deng's critics were seemingly justified in charging him with returning China to social conditions that existed in the early 19th century. If this accusation is valid, then one must ask whether a similar trade union movement will follow, and how long it will take.

The right to strike was enshrined in the 1954 constitution, but this right was taken away when the constitution was amended in 1982, on the grounds that because the proletariat were the masters of this state, they would only be striking against themselves. Chinese workers, which at that time meant those in state-owned factories, had to belong to the All-China Federation of Trade Unions (ACFTU). No other trade unions were or have ever been allowed to exist. Yet the migrant laborers rarely enroll in the official union. In effect, what has happened in Shenzhen is that the state has allowed nonunionized workers to take away jobs from expensive union workers.

Workers both inside and outside the ACFTU do go on strike, even though they break the law when they do so. Still, a couple of hours by bus from Dongguan, I traveled to Shenzhen to meet some girls who had just taken part in a successful strike in November 2005 at the Hai Yan Compuline Factory, which makes DVDs and CD players for export.

The Hai Yan factory is interspersed among middle-class housing developments and brightly lit shopping malls. There are many other

Eight thousand workers are employed at this Guangdong Province shoe factory. If China is now experiencing an industrial revolution like Europe's of the 19th century, can trade unions be far behind?

factories here; Hai Yan shares a gate with Le Conte Chocolate Factory. As I arrived, I encountered a strange scene: Shenzhen's white-collar class was out enjoying Saturday evening shopping or dining while troupes of pale, small girls dressed in work uniforms of different colors walked arm and arm, going on or off shift.

Outside the Hai Yan factory gate, I ran into a man who had seen the strike. "About a thousand girls blocked the traffic on this street for about six hours," he said. Then he added, "You can be sure it was all started by outside agitators."

It was such an odd comment that it made me look at him twice. He turned out to be the manager of Hai Yan's personnel bureau and insisted he had joined the company only after the strike. I asked him whether the strikers had won. "Well, they got a raise from 610 to 690 yuan a month," he said cautiously.

It then took me a long time to find a Compuline worker who confirmed that he was lying. Many of the girls I approached seemed too frightened to talk, but finally I stopped one braver than the others.

"I was there," a girl older than the rest spoke up. "We had to strike. We were only getting paid 230 yuan a month, a third the legal minimum. We sometimes had to work from noon to 2:00 a.m. and there was no limit on overtime."

Now the factory's 2,000 workers are getting 870 yuan a month, 25 percent above the legal minimum. The story of how this dispute unfolded fell into a common pattern. First the workers tried petitioning the factory managers, then they went to the government-run Labor Bureau, and after that they tried every official within reach. When all else failed, they took to the streets. Blocking traffic was one option, and the last resort was to head down to the party headquarters.

In this case, the protests won the attention of the deputy governor of Shenzhen before the protests escalated to the final stage. The authorities fined the company 1.9 million yuan on the grounds that it had failed to pay the statutory minimum wage of 690 yuan. The police also arrested seven of the women strike leaders for breaking the law by going on strike and holding an unauthorized protest.

Other strikes in Shenzhen ran on for a week until the police intervened. One of Shenzhen's biggest strikes took place in 2005 when

Workers at a garment factory in Shenzhen, Guangdong Province. Poor working conditions and inadequate pay plague workers throughout China. Strikes, although illegal, do occur, but the concessions gained are rarely impressive or lasting.

more than 10,000 workers at the Japanese UNIDEM Electronics Products Factory laid down their tools. The factory, which assembles cordless phones for export, paid workers just 480 yuan a month for an 11-hour shift.

This strike was unusual in other respects. The workers were so organized that they sent a collective petition to the factory management listing 15 demands. They wanted to be allowed to set up a trade union at the factory, a concession that had already been agreed to by UNIDEM management in 2000. They wanted sick leave and maternity payments equal to 60 percent of normal wages. The workers currently received no pay at these times; indeed, they often had to pay employers "living allowance" fines. In addition, the UNIDEM workers demanded that, in accordance with China's labor law, workers with ten or more years of seniority should be offered permanent contracts, that no arbitrary dismissals should take place, and that the quality of meals and the water supply in the workers' hostel should be improved.

At length the Japanese management gave in, but as soon as the strike was over, the factory appointed a new manager who ignored the earlier agreement and refused to allow a trade union. Just why is revealing: Factory management said that it had to comply with local laws and that it had come under pressure from the government. In short, the Communist Party was preventing the workers from enjoying basic labor rights, for fear that if it gave in to one group of workers, everyone would want the same.

In Shenzhen, I met Liu Kaiming, a local journalist who had specialized in covering labor issues. He had become so outraged by what he saw in factories that he set up his own nongovernmental organization (NGO), the Institute of Contemporary Observation, to do something about it. A short, wiry, bespectacled man, Liu said that in 2005 there were more than a thousand strikes reported in Shenzhen each involving at least a hundred workers and many more that were never reported. "Many take place secretly because the workers and the management don't want the government to know," he said.

Many of the disputes start because the authorities fail to enforce their own laws and regulations. According to his own research, only 50 percent of the ten million migrants working in Guangdong get the minimum wage and 30 percent are paid less. Chinese labor laws limit the working week to 40 hours, but in practice 95 percent of workers put in a 72-hour week. Overtime is supposed to be paid at triple the normal rate, but Liu said many workers are unsure if or how they are paid for overtime.

There was more. More than 25 million workers in China are now in regular contact with life-threatening toxic dust and poisonous material. China leads the world in reported industrial accidents. Across China, some 728,000 workers are injured and 120,000 die a year. Shenzhen alone reports that some 10,000 migrant workers are injured at work every year and the authorities reckon that ten million workers are exposed to potential health hazards at work. More than 90 percent of occupational injuries occur to migrant workers but only one in five have any accident insurance. It is the norm, Liu said, for factories to decline to take responsibility for occupational injuries.

Before Liu could finish reciting this depressing catalogue of statistical misery, I asked him how it was that migrant workers could be treated so badly. He leaned forward, eager to explain an issue that he complained many foreigners always found hard to grasp.

In the 1950s, the Communist Party created a rural apartheid, registering peasants as a separate class that was excluded from the welfare system granted to the urban and industrial working class. Without this household registration, or *hukou,* a peasant could not live or work in a city without special permission. It was one of the means by which the Communist state extracted wealth from the countryside to finance China's industrialization.

The very first migrant workers were hired in Sichuan Province in 1984 and brought to Shenzhen to work on construction sites. In the 20 years since then, between 90 million and 120 million peasants have become "migrant workers," leaving their homes in search of work. The label is misleading. Few of them are in fact ever allowed to "migrate" and transfer their registration. This situation means that while Shenzhen has 700,000 legal workers, it has eight million temporary migrant workers who have no choice but to return to the countryside after a few years or they become illegal immigrants who could be arrested and jailed at any time.

The Industrial Revolution spurred the rapid urbanization of Great Britain. Although the new English proletariat may have been forced to live in overcrowded slums, they never faced such institutional discrimination. It is true that China is urbanizing fast, but the link between this urbanization and the employment of migrant workers in Dongguan factories is weak.

The low social status of anyone with a rural hukou was illustrated by a case reported in the press in 2005. A fully loaded truck in Chongqing Province collided with a truck carrying three girls, with fatal results. The truck company paid out 200,000 yuan in compensation to the families of two girls but only 58,000 yuan to the third family. The father of the third girl, a butcher, had only a rural registration and the regulations stipulated the much lower compensation for peasants.

The hukou system allows factory owners to avoid paying not only compensation for injuries but even wages. In 2003, the state admitted that the migrant workforce was owed a total of some 60 billion dollars and launched a campaign to force employers to pay back wages.

China's rise as an economic power is, therefore, based on the nearest thing to unpaid labor. Migrant workers can even be cheaper than prison labor. In 1996, I came across prison factories in Shenyang, in Northeast China, that had been forced to close down because they could not compete with the prices of goods produced in Guangdong factories.

Some factories in Dongguan, like the Taiwan-invested Debao Handbag Factory, have even made claims that it was their employees who owed *them* money. The handbag factory deducted 40 yuan for food and board and a labor fee of 30 yuan, which left its workers with a net weekly wage of just 75 yuan. The workers staged protests in March 2005. Then in September 2005, just six months after the Debao protests, 250 workers from the Zhiye Shoe Factory blocked a road in the Baiyun District of Guangzhou. The management deducted so much money from their wages that the factory said the workers each owed 80 yuan at the end of the month.

It is hard to find a more docile and industrious people than the Chinese peasants, but Liu Kaiming said attitudes are beginning to harden. The first migrant workers came from provinces like Sichuan where millions had perished from starvation in the Great Leap Forward (1958–1962) and the survivors spent the following two decades in grim hardship. It was not surprising that they grasped at any opportunity. If they didn't, there were 200 or 300 others ready to step into their shoes.

In Britain's industrial revolution wages and conditions steadily improved, but not in China's—at least not yet. In fact, they have declined in real terms. Since 1990, the cost of living has risen by a factor of three or four; measured in cash terms, migrant wages are much the same or lower.

It is hard for peasants to organize themselves and use their numbers for collective bargaining when even China's privileged classes are forbidden to associate freely. And the hukou system means that when a worker is fired, he loses any legal right to continue living in Shenzhen. "Once they leave home, they are as vulnerable as a snail without a shell," Liu said. Most do not even have legal employment contracts, so winning a court case is hard. Liu's organization has helped some groups fight for their rights, but the time and money required is so great that most peasants just give up and return home in defeat. His institute has been very active in doing what it can. It has set up internal complaints mechanisms in 500 factories, conducted social audits in 200 plants, and helped more than 10,000 workers in their disputes.

One reason why Dongguan factory owners do not treat their workers better is that profit margins are often very low. In 19th-cen-

One of the worst aspects of China's labor environment is the frequency of major and minor workplace accidents. These men are former employees of toy and computer factories in southern China who lost limbs on the job and then were fired; retribution is limited.

tury Britain, mill owners quickly became very wealthy by adopting new manufacturing technology. Liu thinks that in Dongguan competition is so fierce that profit margins rarely rise above 5 percent. It is too easy for anyone to buy some machines and hire a few workers, so there is no room to maneuver. Take the toy industry. China has 6,000 manufacturers, and a third of them belong to Hong Kong companies who supply the likes of Mattel, Hasbro, and Disney. China now makes 70 percent of the world's toys, and its exports are worth some eight billion dollars a year.

Monina Wong, a researcher with the Hong Kong Coalition for the Charter on the Safe Production of Toys, explained the economics behind a Barbie doll sold by Mattel. It retails in American shops for 10 dollars, and of that, eight dollars goes to transportation, marketing, retailing, wholesalers, and profit for Mattel. Of the remaining two dollars, one dollar is shared by the management and shippers in Hong Kong and 65 cents is spent on raw materials from Taiwan, Japan, the United States, and Saudi Arabia. The remaining 35 cents goes to the factory in China, which must cover the cost of labor, electricity, and owning the factory.

So although the manufacturing has moved to Dongguan, the profits remain with the foreign company that owns the brands and the technology. It is the same with textiles, apparel, and even high-tech products like computers or mobile phones. Textile firms employ 19 million workers and in 2005 produced 408 billion dollars' worth of products—so each employee generates a mere $21 in value in a year.

Many foreign companies have moved production to China not just in search of cheaper labor but also to take advantage of the absence of unions and labor legislation. May Wong of the Asia Monitor Resource Centre said Hong Kong toy manufacturers moved out of Hong Kong and switched production away from countries like Thailand and Indonesia in preference to China. "One of the main reasons they moved to China was the increase in workers' activism in those other countries," she said. Thailand's toy industry had been growing handsomely in the late 1980s, but by the mid-1990s its exports became stuck at one billion dollars and have since been declining.

South Korean manufacturers have become big investors in China to escape the frequent strikes at home. Although workers in factories in Korea work long hours under a similar tight discipline, the trade union movement is strong and fiercely fought strikes are common.

Progress in raising standards in China is slow. Hong Kong researchers like May Wong and Monina Wong joined the effort to improve labor conditions in China after a terrible fire in 1993. The Zhili Toy Factory in Shenzhen, which was making plastic toys for the Italian company Chicco, was swept by a fire that left 87 dead and 47 injured. The workers were trapped by blocked exits and barred windows in dormitories built over the warehouse and factory. It took seven years before the victims received compensation. The company said it would give 1.3 million (Hong Kong) dollars to the workers, but this was never paid because the Chinese court withheld the list of the victims' names. In 1999, the money went to a mainland charity while campaigners struggled to trace the names of the victims and locate 120 families scattered in five provinces. Each family received about 10,000 yuan in compensation. Meanwhile, the Hong Kong–born factory owner, who was jailed for two years, reopened another factory and is still producing toys for Chicco.

In the two centuries since the Lancashire mills opened, labor costs have fallen to an ever smaller share of the final price of many products. One day it might disappear altogether. The timing of China's entry into the global economy seems to have been a stroke of luck. A crack in history opened up. Had China delayed its Open Door policy, robot technology might have advanced far enough for some industries to do without human labor altogether.

Many of China's exports in the 17th and 19th centuries, like porcelain, were produced by highly skilled workmen hand-painting vases. As the Industrial Revolution spread to more industries, the losers were skilled craftsmen. In the machine age, companies like Ford made ever more complicated products like cars, but production depended on clusters of factories employing a pool of skilled workers. By the 1980s, car manufacturers began to promise that even these were about to be replaced. The Italian carmaker Fiat produced a stylishly choreographed advertisement boasting its latest models were

"Handbuilt by Robots." The new industry promised to make the skilled factory worker extinct.

The Japanese led the investment craze in robots and computer-integrated manufacturing. The first boom turned to bust at the end of the 1980s. Many U.S. manufacturers, including the auto industry, discovered that robots are expensive and hard to install. Instead, companies began to drive down costs by outsourcing parts from East Asia, especially from the "tiger economies" of Taiwan, South Korea, Hong Kong, and Singapore. In South Korea's sweatshops, workers worked just as long hours as those in China today.

As wages rose in South Korea and the other tigers, the outsourcing companies began moving production into China, creating a complicated global supply chain. There are now, for instance, more than 57,000 Taiwanese firms in Dongguan, and 110,000 Taiwanese live there with their own schools, hospitals, and clubs.

The Japanese stuck with the robot revolution for a while. Many companies preferred to keep investing in automated production to off-set the rising cost of domestic labor and the appreciation of the yen. With their tradition of guaranteed lifetime employment, Japanese companies tried to stay ahead by becoming ever more capital intensive. Japan became home to 40 percent of the 750,000 robots in daily operation around the world. The result was that when the Japanese economy stumbled in the 1990s, growth stagnated and unemployment rose while the American high-tech sector boomed. One factor was the entrance of China's huge and cheap labor force into the world economy. The development caught industrialists in Tokyo by surprise, and U.S. high-tech companies who relied on Chinese assembly workers regained lost ground. By this time, it had also become clear, even to the Japanese, that robots are often less useful than had been expected. Robots were best employed in a handful of industries like auto manufacturing to do a few jobs like spot welding.

You can use robots on production lines to make personal computers, mobile phones, and cameras, but at the speed at which new products are developed, it is cheaper and easier to employ humans. They are simply more flexible than machines. It could take six months to reprogram and recalibrate a completely automated production line for a new camera, but only an afternoon might be needed to reorganize a human workforce to solder together the new product.

Computer chips doubled in capacity every 18 months, making it possible to pack more and more features onto a product. As the time frame between new and better products shrank, this flexibility became ever more important. Manufacturers wanted to bring out a new product quickly before it became obsolete. If it sold well, a factory could quickly expand production by hiring more workers, but if it flopped, the workers could be immediately fired. Some manufacturers even found that their human workforce made better quality products with fewer defects than the computerized robots. In the end, many Japanese companies were belatedly forced to shift production to China.

The cost-effectiveness of Chinese labor has inspired many companies to move their assembly operations to China. Here, Nissan "Sunny" cars are being assembled at a plant of the Dongfeng-Nissan joint venture in Guangdong Province.

All this explains why in 2005 China overtook the United States as the world's largest exporter of computers and other high-tech electronic products. And why it is a less impressive feat than it sounds.

Still, although the 1980s hype about robots may have been premature, Japanese companies like Toyota say that the new generation of robots will soon bring domestic production costs down to "Chinese levels." The Japanese newspaper *Nihon Keizai Shimbun* reported in 2004 that new robots developed with Yaskawa Electric Corporation can handle multiple tasks simultaneously with two arms and achieve production efficiencies equal to or better than human workers. Just when "lights out" factories making cars handbuilt by robots will become commonplace is hard to predict, but it is possible to imagine a near future when even the cheapest unskilled Chinese peasants will become redundant.[1]

Technology is changing assumptions about the future of industrial labor needs. Recent studies suggest that the link between high growth and job creation may not continue forever. The Asian Development Bank estimates that in the 1980s it took a 3 percent increase in economic growth to produce a 1 percent increase in employment. By the 1990s it took more than twice as much growth—a 7.8 percent increase—to achieve the same result. "What we've seen in many countries in Asia is that growth used to have a very strong relationship with employment," said Lawrence Jeff Johnson, the chief analyst of employment trends at the International Labor Organization (ILO). "It doesn't anymore."[2]

And one must ask the question: For how much longer will Chinese labor remain so cheap and plentiful? The first signs of a shortage of workers appeared in 2003; shoe factories in Quanzhou, Fujian Province, reported difficulties in finding enough female workers. By spring 2004, shortages forced more than 20 percent of the Quanzhou factories to either close or move. The shortages spread to other parts of southern China where export-processing factories are concentrated. By the end of 2004, officials were talking of a shortfall of some six million to eight million workers.

Demography explains why in the medium term the available workforce must shrink as China's population ages. Chairman Mao encouraged families to have male children after the Great Leap

Forward famine. Those born in the mid-1960s began entering the labor market in the mid-1980s. At the time they were getting married, the party began to rigidly enforce its one-child policy. The next generation will be smaller, so the available pool of young peasant girls is bound to shrink.

Experts like Liu Kaiming believe the labor shortages in 2004 were a temporary blip caused by low wages, and he points out that the shortages did not lead to real wage hikes. The shortages came about because the companies making clothing, shoes, electronics, and toys were expanding faster than news of the jobs reached villages in central and western China. In rural China some 200 million are still short of jobs. China could create another 36 million jobs for unskilled peasant girls before facing real shortages.

Could this scenario happen? Chinese economic planners seem confident that China can and will continue to attract high rates of foreign investment for another ten years and that it will double or triple its exports. Yet there are other factors at work. Chinese factory wages are already significantly higher than countries in the region like Sri Lanka, Myanmar, Indonesia, Vietnam, Laos, and Cambodia. Secondly, Beijing is committed to allowing the yuan to float. Some economists argue that it has been undervalued against the dollar since 1994 by as much as 30 or 40 percent.

In addition, there is growing pressure from both inside and outside the country to adapt labor regulations to meet international standards. "We are in a pre-union phase like in 19th-century Europe," said Robin Munro, research director for the *China Labour Bulletin,* a Hong Kong–based NGO that monitors labor rights in China from Hong Kong. "There is a mounting awareness of labor rights. Five years ago there was no labor movement. Now it is building all over country." Liu Kaiming also believes that attitudes among the workers are changing. "This is a new generation in the workforce. They haven't known starvation like their parents and they grew up in a more open China, more aware of their rights," he said.

So far Dongguan factories are required to submit to only voluntary codes of conduct set by foreign companies concerned about their customer image. Organizations like Liu's Institute of Contemporary

Observation carry out the audits despite doubts about their effectiveness.

"What goes on with companies is a cat-and-mouse game," said Munro. Monitors arrive at factories once or twice a year and for a few hours check the books, time sheets, and salaries. "The factory owners know how to run rings around the inspectors, produce fake time sheets, and even coach the workers to give the correct answers."

The *New York Times* saw a memo of one company that ordered workers to "intentionally waste time and then say they can't find them"[3] when monitors asked to see documentation of employee pensions, medical insurance, and work contracts.

In the end, codes of conduct that companies like Reebok use cannot be a substitute for worker participation. "They won't work as long as workers are not involved and that won't happen until there are real unions," Munro said. The time when migrant workers are able to form independent trade unions could still be a long way off, according to Liu. "Workers rarely understand the need for unions, but we can change things. We are educating them about their rights," he said.

On paper, Chinese labor laws and regulations are liberal enough, and activists are now trying to get them actually implemented. For example, recent legislation gives workers the right to negotiate collective contracts and elect their own representatives. Only a small minority of companies sign any contracts with their workers, however, and it is hard for workers to sue their employers in court and win.

Guangzhou regulations grant that migrant workers living in

Guangdong for seven years straight may apply for a hukou or permanent residency, provided they first possess a temporary residence permit. However, this arrangement is a catch-22; migrant workers rarely obtain temporary residence permits for seven years running.

Much also depends on the willingness of local governments to enforce laws. Often officials have reasons to delay implementing reforms. A local government that raises labor costs by enforcing labor laws risks seeing the factories move either abroad or to other parts of China. Government budgets and official salaries depend on keeping the factory owners happy.

One of the peculiar features of China's modernization is that local governments appear to have become richer than the capitalist investors. The government of Shenzhen, where there are eight million migrant workers, in 2004 earned the sum of 118 billion yuan (15 billion dollars) from the taxes it levied on the local factories. Most of this is remitted to the central government, but Shenzhen keeps a third for itself. In addition, Shenzhen has earned substantial but unreported sums from the sale of land leases.

"The Shenzhen government doesn't have to give a penny to the migrant workers although they create all the wealth," Liu Kaiming pointed out. Instead, Shenzhen has been able to create a modern First World infrastructure and pay its officials generous salaries and perks.

The resistance to change the labor laws is deep rooted and even extends to Hong Kong. Some of its leading tycoons, like Sir Gordon Wu, have spoken out against introducing a directly elected government in Hong Kong because they claim it would damage Hong Kong's economic competitiveness. They fear that politicians would woo the electorate by creating welfare states like those in Western Europe, where business is plagued by excessive regulation, high wages, labor immobility, shorter working hours, and high health costs. They warn the result would be high unemployment and slower growth.

If China were to become a democracy tomorrow, a big majority of the electorate would be peasants and migrant workers who would inevitably demand equal rights and higher wages. Average incomes in Shenzhen are 5,000 dollars per year (and some 3,000 dollars per year for urban residents in Guangdong Province as a whole) or more than 500

Employment assistance for laid-off workers is just one of China's relatively generous, if laxly enforced, labor regulations. Here a woman listens to a recruitment session in Guangzhou that's part of the reemployment program offered by the local government.

times higher than that of the migrant workers. But if migrant workers had the same voting rights in Shenzhen as residents, they would outvote them eight to one.

China's strategy of development, its high economic growth rates, and the future evolution of its political system hinge on the migrant worker issue. However, raising the status of the vast billion-strong peasant underclass involves social change on an equally vast scale.

China was granted membership in the WTO after a major debate in the United States and other countries around the world. Many argued that trade and investment will promote that change by opening society to democratic values, including workers' rights. However, the WTO agreement with China excluded any social clauses, so trade is not conditional on human rights progress.

China has also joined the ILO and became a member of its governing body. It has still not, however, ratified the ILO's core conventions, including those on the freedom of association, the right to organize, and the right of workers to bargain collectively for improvements in their working conditions. While China ratified the UN's International Covenant on Economic, Social, and Cultural Rights, it entered a reservation on blocking the application of a clause to the treaty guaranteeing workers the right to form and join trade unions of their choice.

It is true that China is beginning to dismantle the hukou system, gradually removing the restrictions that have prevented peasants from moving to the cities and finding jobs. Cities like Beijing, which until 2000 had regulations that barred hiring migrants for more than 100 kinds of jobs, are slowly lifting the restrictions. A new campaign to raise health and safety standards in factories and to make injury insurance mandatory is also under way.

The key to sustaining Shenzhen's and China's economic growth is to slowly raise the living standards of migrant workers.

The government is forcing employers to pay back wages and is trying to raise living standards in the countryside by reducing taxes. It needs to create a consumer economy and to rely more on domestic demand rather than exports to power the economy. The next chapter looks at how the rural economy has been faring under the reforms.

When Deng Xiaoping launched the SEZs, he promised his followers that they would be vehicles to import new technology and management techniques. With one or two exceptions, this has not happened, but the story is far from over. While there are almost no Chinese companies in the high-tech field nor any well-known Chinese brands, China is beginning to create successful companies that manufacture high-end consumer products like cars. So far, Chinese manufacturers have become better known for the theft of intellectual property. They produce more than 60 percent of knockoffs in the world and foreign companies are complaining loudly. So are workers in countries with high labor costs and elaborate welfare systems. Deng's revolution continues, and the ripples are spreading all across the world.

CENTRAL CHINA

AGRICULTURAL LIFE AND THE INITIATION OF REFORMS

CHAPTER SIX

Fengyang, a typical farming county in Anhui Province, is famous in China for its beggars. It is the birthplace of the most able beggar of all, Zhu Yuanzhang, who went on to found the great Ming dynasty. The traditions have not died. Peasants from Fengyang still head every year to Shanghai to beg, and I have met some of them on the steps of the Astor Hotel, telling tales of crops ruined by floods or droughts.

Ten years ago I visited Fengyang to research a book, *Hungry Ghosts,* on the Great Leap Forward famine, which cost some 30 million lives across China between 1958 and 1962. I chose to visit Fengyang for two reasons: First, horrific details of the famine in Fengyang had been revealed in a book published in China based on documents from the local party archives; and, second, Fengyang was one of the places where China's rural reforms began just after Chairman Mao Zedong's death in 1976.

On that 1996 visit, I talked to people at random as long as they were old enough to have experienced the famine firsthand: peasants working in the fields, a woman running a roadside restaurant, villagers in their homes, and local officials who invited me to a fancy lunch. Everyone talked candidly of their own experiences and what had happened when a third of the population perished of hunger. And they talked, too, with satisfaction about how much they now had to eat. Every household had a reserve of grain, stored in baskets or a small granary at the back of the yard.

China's agricultural interior holds great beauty—most famously in the fabled landscape around Guilin, depicted here—though the country's growing prosperity has barely registered beyond the urban centers.

PREVIOUS PAGES
A little girl in an Anhui Province village. The billion peasants of rural China have seen centuries of misery, but better days may be ahead for the next generation.

One other thing that struck me was how forthright peasants in China can be compared to city folk, who are far more cautious and schooled in what they should say and think. Even so, these rural people have almost no voice in China. Although rural China is vast—some one billion people scattered over a million villages in an area the size of the United States—not much news about their lives reaches the outside world. What new information has emerged in the decade since I visited Fengyang creates a very bleak picture of growing anger marked by sporadic protests and violent repression.

For instance, two Chinese journalists, Wu Chuntao and her husband Chen Guidi, who traveled through rural Anhui, produced a book, *A Survey of Chinese Peasants* (Zhongguo Nongmin Diaocha), and had this to say: "We have seen unimaginable poverty, unimaginable evil, unimaginable suffering and desperation, unimaginable resistance and silence." The couple had spent three years traveling to more than 50 towns in Anhui Province and interviewing thousands of peasants. Their book was promptly banned by the Chinese government, but some seven million pirated copies were sold in China to readers curious to understand what lay behind the official propaganda.

What, I wondered, has gone so wrong in rural China? If we read any official account of China's "economic miracle," whether written by Chinese scholars or Western economists, it never fails to mention that the reforms have lifted more than 250 million peasants out of absolute poverty. In the 1980s, I witnessed how the peasants prospered and built themselves new houses and started small businesses. Then, in the 1990s, millions of younger peasants left places like Fengyang and found work in factories in places like Dongguan or on construction sites in the big cities. Surely, places like Fengyang ought now to be thriving if only because of the billions of yuan sent home in remittances by these migrant workers. In addition, Anhui Province has reported annual economic growth rates of 9 percent.

When I recently went back to Fengyang for the second time, I hired a taxi in Anhui's capital, Hefei, and we drove down the same pleasant but deserted road. We could have taken a longer route using the new highways that had opened, but we would not have saved any time. Along the way, the countryside looked much the same, apart from the new

Wuhu, in Anhui Province, has grown in recent years, but there is too little money in the region for a real boom.

building. Everyone seemed to be replacing the housing thrown up in the 1980s with more comfortable homes, usually a square two-story concrete block with a flat roof. Arriving in Fengyang, it seemed bigger and more prosperous. Many more shops and restaurants had opened and there were now two traffic lights needed to regulate the traffic. Clearly quite a number of people had moved into town from the surrounding villages, but on the other hand there was little foreign investment. No factories had opened up and there was still not a decent hotel.

Rural inland provinces like Anhui capture only a small percentage of China's foreign investment. On my first visit, the villagers had pleaded with me to invest in a factory, imagining that I could somehow conjure up a gleaming car plant on my own.

In Fengyang, the biggest boost to the local economy seems to have come from a new gravel pit, and big trucks carrying the rocks were the only commercial traffic on the road. In other parts of the province, like the nearby city of Bengbu, some chemical factories had sprung up, but with mixed blessings. The pollution from chemical factories had ruined the Huai River, killing off the fish and spoiling the crops.

The ruins of Ming dynasty founder Zhu Yuanzhang's first capital, Zhongdu, are just outside Fengyang and are being restored as a tourist attraction. When I was here ten years earlier, local officials spoke of their great plans to develop Fengyang as a profitable tourist center, but not much had been achieved. The first thing I did was to go back to revisit the historic sights. There was still not a lot to see in the town, apart from a city gate preserved in the center, which was still being restored, and some fake old-looking shopping arcades. Outside the town, the high walls of Zhongdu were visible from the road rising above the flat fields, but the driver told me the track leading to them was too muddy to drive.

The main tourist attraction was a little farther on. As a dutiful son, Zhu had recovered the remains of his parents, who had both died of starvation. He had posthumously declared his mother to be the empress of Chun and built her an imposing imperial tomb. It was raining hard that day, so I was the only visitor to walk past the grand spirit avenue—a line of stone statues of generals, officials, lions, and horses—to the huge tree-covered mound enshrining Zhu's parents. Since my last visit, the authorities had tidied it up and now charged visitors a 30-yuan entrance fee.

The Chinese are traditionally said to view history as a repetition of cycles, while Western history books usually present history as a narrative of gradual progress and enlightenment. In the past century, the Chinese, too, have created a similar narrative for themselves. Since the fall of the Qing dynasty, Chinese history has always been presented as a march of progress, a narrative that shapes the current government's daily propaganda and its presentation of the five-year economic plans. The Chinese purport that by 2050 they will have built a modern prosperous state and will be enjoying the standard of living enjoyed by middle-income nations. By then, the population will be in decline and China will be an urban, industrialized society with a modern welfare state.

As I walked around the tomb clutching my dripping umbrella, I wondered which view was the more credible. The whole history of Fengyang seems to bear out the traditional Chinese view in which each dynasty completes the same cycle as the last one.

After the Mongols had completed their conquest of China, peasants in central China were driven to revolt by harsh taxes and food shortages. Like other Fengyang peasants before and after him, Zhu Yuanzhang, a determined man with a face like a pig (or so his contemporaries said), had to leave his home. Soon he joined a Buddhist sect with millenarian beliefs that organized an armed uprising against the Mongol Yuan dynasty. Zhu emerged as a leader of a force known as the Red Turbans because of their distinctive headgear. When the Mongol dynasty was overthrown, Zhu named himself the new emperor of China and in 1368 established the Ming dynasty. Zhu set about creating a new utopian social order, but as he grew older he became a paranoid tyrant who ordered horrifyingly violent purges of his followers. When he died, his successor abandoned dreams of creating a new, more just society and even moved the court out of the great city Zhu had built at Nanjing.

After 250 years, the Ming dynasty collapsed when the country was torn apart by peasant uprisings provoked by harsh taxes and food shortages. The leaders of the peasant rebel armies lost out when from the north the warlike Manchus took advantage of the internal chaos and crossed the Great Wall. They established the Qing dynasty in Beijing, which lasted from 1644 to 1911.

Mao Zedong's life parallels that of Zhu Yuanzhang's so closely that it seems uncanny: a peasant leader, a rebellion against foreign invaders, military conquest, a new dynasty promising a utopian social order, and a descent into tyranny, purges, and mass starvation. Mao loved reading histories of the Ming dynasty, and both he and his followers were all too aware of the parallels with Zhu. The start of the Cultural Revolution was marked by an attack on an opera about an upright Ming dynasty mandarin who dared to chastise the emperor for policies that were causing great hunger.

What if all the revolutions and upheavals of the 20th century had in the end brought little change to life in rural China? It is radical, even shocking, to suggest that a century of modernization has changed little for most Chinese. Yet an internal party document leaked in Hong Kong in 1998 would seem to offer support for that idea. Based on an internal party investigation, the document published as an "internal reference report" noted that between the winter of 1996 and the spring of 1997, a total of 380,000 peasants in 36 counties in 9 provinces, including Anhui, had taken part in riots and demonstrations. Some local party and government cadres had even encouraged the peasants to demonstrate and personally participated in the processions. The protesters had put forward slogans like "Down

with the urban bureaucratic exploiting class" and "Share the wealth of new local overlords in the countryside and establish peasants' own political power."[1]

In Anhui itself, more than 70,000 peasants in 50 market towns had held rallies and delivered petitions. The protesters had raided party and government buildings, ransacked files, and seized the guns and ammunition of the armed police. On one occasion, 500 peasants had blocked a freight train, seized the cargo, and clashed with railway police. More than 40 people were injured and 11 died, including 5 public security guards and policemen.

Since then, the protests have continued and grown: The New York–based nongovernmental organization Human Rights in China reported in September 2003, drawing on another internal party document, that more than three million people took part in protests and demonstrations in just one month.[2] In more than a hundred cases across China, the protests escalated into large and violent clashes between demonstrators and local police in which government buildings were torched.

On the way back from the ruins and the tomb, I stopped off at one roadside house to see whether the residents could confirm these reports. I found the Lu family shivering in a shell of building with no windows, doors, or heating. It was a new house and they had been trying to find the money to finish it for the last five years. Mr. Lu, a tough, strong-looking man, talked about his life with an air of resignation. "We are still very poor here. You can't make a living from farming."

He confirmed that in recent years, many farmers in Fengyang had joined together to protest unfair taxes. Thousands of them had driven their tractors down to the local government offices in town. Too many officials were corrupt and paying the farmers too little for the grain, he said.

The Lu family ought to have been relatively well off. Mr. Lu had gone to work as a watchman at a university campus in Guangdong back in 1987, while his wife stayed at home to farm their small plot of land. Later, their two children left to work in export-processing factories in the south. "All the young people have left. They have all gone south to look for work. There is nothing to do here," he explained.

The daughter worked in a garment factory in Hangzhou and only

Relentless poverty in the rural provinces has not allowed much modernization, and even five-year-olds must work.

came home at Spring Festival. This was the only time in the year she saw her two children, three and six years old, and her husband. In the meantime, her parents looked after her children.

Even so, in spite of an individuals' hard work, in Fengyang County the average annual income for a peasant is about 1,000 yuan, or just $125. For all the explosive growth of China's manufacturing exports, China remains an agricultural country where most people earn their living from the land. More than a third of them live below the World Bank's definition of poverty, meaning they earn less than a dollar day.

Farther along the road, past one of the small Protestant churches common in this area, I went to talk to the Chus. The five members of the Chu family relied on income from growing rice and wheat on six mu (just under an acre) of land. They, too, were living in a shell of a new house that they said had cost them about 40,000 yuan (5,000 dollars), and it boasted an old black-and-white TV set flickering in a corner.

"However hard we work, we just can't get rich. It is the taxes. There are too many of them," complained Mr. Chu, who was some 20 years younger than Mr. Lu. He had two children at school and also had to pay heavy school fees. Medical bills were another problem. If anyone fell sick, the doctor's fees were so high that the expense could ruin the whole family. In short, despite working hard, neither family was earning enough from farming or laboring work to escape poverty.

Mr. Chu thought he knew how to solve the poverty. "Why don't you build a factory here?" he suggested. "Many people don't have work here, and the land is cheap." It was the same idea that everyone had raised on my first visit ten years earlier.

I asked both families about the nearby church. This part of Anhui has been a stronghold of Christianity since the 1920s. Most of the believers are poorer peasants and many are Protestants, but they belong to unofficial and indigenous churches like the Shouters, so known because the adherents are encouraged to shout their devotion. In northern Anhui, Mr. Chu explained that the unrest is sometimes mixed up with protests against the Communist Party's attempts to suppress these unofficial churches.

The state has tried to stifle the growth of recognized religion, and sects such as the Established King Network, the Born Again Movement, and the Total Scope Church, which were often founded by local peasants based on their own interpretation of the Bible. The religious movements offer the hard-pressed peasants hope and promises of salvation, and they tap into a long Chinese tradition of secret societies and religious cults dating back at least to the Mongols. In China, the only way to organize resistance to the all-powerful state has been to join a secret society or cult.

To understand why Chinese peasants should want to organize resistance against the Communist Party, which supposedly represents them and came to power on the back of peasant anger against the corruption and oppression of the Nationalists, one needs to go back to the 1950s. Chairman Mao promised to redistribute land holdings to his followers and soon after winning power organized the deaths of millions of "landlords" in local kangaroo courts. The peasants did not get to keep the fields for long, however. Impatient at the slow pace of change in the countryside, Mao launched the Great Leap Forward in 1958, promising to realize communism overnight, industrialize China, overtake Great Britain, and catch up to the United States.

New farming techniques, copied from the Soviet Union and based on the theories of bogus scientists like Trofim Lysenko, were introduced. The Communists promised that these advances would triple or even quadruple grain harvests and there would be so much food that a third of the fields could be used to grow flowers. Mao was shown experimental fields where wheat grew so densely packed that children could lie on top. Leading officials outdid each other in reporting the success of such innovations as digging deep furrows and planting crops close together and reported yields a thousand times, even 20,000 times, higher than normal.

Peasants lost all their land and had to join people's communes modeled on Soviet collective farms. They had to give all their livestock, farm tools, and even their pots and pans to the communes. This collectivization was why they were so poor in 1976. They had literally lost all of their possessions. They were also forbidden to cook at home and had to eat in communal kitchens. Men and women were marched to and from work like soldiers and were paid in "work points" instead of money.

As the birthplace of Zhu Yuanzhang, Fengyang had been singled out and given one of the first tractor stations in the country. The heavy Soviet tractors were imported to till the giant fields that were created by amalgamating private farms. Anhui Province was turned into a model for communist rural reforms, and its party secretary, Zeng Xisheng, was fanatical about establishing the people's communes and abolishing all private property.

For thousands of years Chinese peasants had had to deliver taxes to the emperor in the form of grain. This food surplus was used to feed the court and the army and to supply the cities. Some was used to supply peasants with food when in winter they were obliged to contribute a month or two of corvée labor to work on irrigation projects and other kinds of public works. Some of it was stored in public granaries to be distributed in times of famine or natural disasters.

Normally, the grain tax was set at a quarter of the harvest. Based on Anhui's exaggerated harvest figures, which became ever more inflated as the figures were reported up the hierarchy, local officials levied a far higher grain tax. In effect, Mao and his followers levied a 100 percent grain tax and forced the peasants into year-round corvée labor, such as making steel or digging dams. In many places across China, officials tried to extract from peasants several times the actual harvest.

To force people to hand over food that did not exist, they carried out house-to-house searches, trying to find hidden stores. If nothing was found, officials would torture or beat the peasants and take livestock or other possessions as substitutes. Although huge numbers of people starved to death, there was in fact enough food stored in state granaries to feed the population.

The grandmother of the Chu family, a bent old woman with silver hair, vividly recalled those days. "We had to eat cabbage roots and tree leaves. Our family survived by secretly growing vegetables," she said. "In most places, 30 percent of population died. Every family lost a couple of people. A lot of girls died and many people ran away. They disappeared and didn't come back for many years. I remember a lot of people died on this road trying to get to Fengyang where they thought there was food. They fell down the road, and then they were too weak to get up and walk anymore."

Chinese peasants are no strangers to famine—these victims are getting much needed rice in 1946—but the starvation caused by the Great Leap Forward in 1958–62 was the worst ever.

No emperor in Chinese history had abused the imperial system as savagely as Mao. He was not motivated, however, by avarice but by a belief that there was a shortcut to modernization. In the Soviet Union, Joseph Stalin had financed a crash industrialization program by squeezing the countryside and causing several great famines. Mao decided he could do the same but on an even grander scale.

As the state tried to force through huge increases in output, Mao brought some 20 million peasants into the cities to work on an accelerated industrial expansion program. It soon ended in utter economic ruin. Most of the steel produced turned out to be useless lumps of metal. There was nothing left to eat or wear and even 20 years later many peasants still had not recovered. The peasant-workers were sent home, and soon the cities had to be emptied for there was no way of feeding the inhabitants. During the 1960s and 1970s, some 70 million to 90 million urban cadres and "educated youths" were dispatched to the countryside. The proportion of China's population living in cities fell to just 15 percent, the lowest in Chinese history and the lowest rate of any nation in the world.

After Mao's death in 1976, Chinese scholars chose to investigate Fengyang's local party archives to understand what had actually happened and produced a 600-page book, *Thirty Years in the Countryside.* It revealed that a quarter of the city's 335,000 inhabitants had starved to death and officials savagely persecuted another 28,000. Some were buried alive, strangled, beaten, tortured, or imprisoned. Many fled and never came back. Across Anhui, the death toll is put at two million and unofficially reported at eight million out of a total population of more than 30 million. This was a man-made catastrophe, indeed a holocaust, greater than in Cambodia or indeed any country. The national death toll of the famine is commonly reckoned to be 30 million, the greatest famine death toll in history.

The new leadership discovered that 250 million people, or one in three peasants, were actually starving. Part of this had to do with a crude accounting trick invented to flatter Mao and to show that his policies worked. The statistics counted sweet potatoes as grain and measured the harvest from the fields. People, however, lived on dried sweet potato chips—which shrink to a tenth of the reported weight. In fact, people had less to eat (and wear) than they had before 1949. In Anhui, agricultural yields had fallen below the levels recorded in the Han dynasty 2,000 years earlier. By comparison, over Mao's 30-year reign, farmers in Japan had raised their productivity 20 times, and South Koreans had improved yields by a factor of 60.

Maoist agriculture was simply not capable of growing and supplying enough food to the cities. That was why Mao had to send a large part of the urban population to live in the countryside. They were told to "learn from the peasants," but in fact they were there just to get something to eat. The peasants did everything they could to resist the Communist Party and its directives. Whenever possible they would eat the crops in the fields before they were harvested, and if that subterfuge did not work they went on a permanent slowdown.

When Mao died and the party could begin cautiously reforming his ideas, the priorities were agriculture and regaining the loyalty of the peasants. The first steps were very cautious. The new party secretary of Anhui, Wan Li, issued six guidelines that allowed peasants to grow vegetables on three-tenths of a mu instead of two-tenths of a mu, and they no longer had to pay taxes on wheat and oil-bearing crops grown on private plots. Small though this gesture was, peasants like the Chu family said they still remembered Wan Li with gratitude. For the first time in years, they had a chance to fill their bellies.

Wan was actually reverting to the temporary measures adopted in Anhui back in 1961 as a means to end the famine. Peasants were allowed to grow food on a tiny private plot of land and to trade the food grown on these plots in local markets. They were also allowed to cook at home again. Even though the communal canteens were abandoned, the peasants continued to spend their days working the fields of the commune as members of huge military-style brigades.

These policies had infuriated Mao, who regarded them as a retreat into capitalism, and he accused those who backed them, men like Liu Shaoqi and Deng Xiaoping, of being "capitalist roaders." This disagreement created a rift within the party so great that, although the famine ended, Mao launched the Cultural Revolution four years later. He violently purged all those, like Deng, who had betrayed the purity of his vision just as Zhu Yuanzhang had done centuries before.

Within months of Mao's death, a new cycle of dynastic history began. A band of peasants in Fengyang secretly agreed to abandon his policies. According to the official party history, the heads of 18 households in a tiny village at Xiaogang in Fengyang County, nearly all of whom shared the name Yan, applied their thumbprints to a secret compact. They secretly divided up the production team's land and distributed the remaining oxen, plows, and agricultural tools among themselves. They began to farm the plots individually. That way, they knew they would have more food to eat. If one or more were caught and jailed, the others swore to raise their neighbor's children.

By the end of 1978, the practice of dividing up communal land into private plots was renamed the "household responsibility system" and adopted as national policy at the third plenum of the 11th Party Congress, the key meeting that saw Deng Xiaoping recognized as China's paramount leader and launched his reforms. Consequently, Xiaogang village is now a tourist attraction in its own right with a little monument recording the bravery of the peasants. Their original contract lies behind a glass case in the Museum of Revolutionary History in Beijing.

The reforms boosted grain production from 286 million tons in 1976 to 407 million tons by 1984, and soon China emerged as a net food exporter for the first time in a generation. At the end of the 1980s, Beijing reported there were just 100 million people left in dire poverty, meaning they could not feed or clothe themselves for at least half the year. More than half of these lived in mountainous areas.

After 1984, the state also freed peasants from the burden of growing

a fixed quota of grain and permitted them to work in nonagricultural enterprises or run their own small businesses, like running food stalls or opening carpentry shops. The luckier ones near the cities began cycling in everyday, ingeniously outfitting their bicycles with devices to transport fresh fish, chickens, vegetables, and fruits. The new cash income spurred everyone to build themselves a new house. Soon the peasants were earning more and living in bigger houses than people in the cities, an unheard-of development in Chinese history.

When the reforms started, the central government was preoccupied with the basic issue of ensuring that citizens had enough to eat. China had once been known as the "land of famine" because mass starvation was a recurrent tragedy. When Deng came to power, he inherited twin problems from Mao: a demographic explosion because Mao had encouraged unrestricted population growth after the famine; and a state grain monopoly needed to guarantee the supply of subsidized basic foods to urban China. Top officials did not dare relax their control over peasant China for fear that if either problem got out of hand, it would derail the entire modernization project. The party and the peasants, therefore, have remained in conflict over two very fundamental issues: population control and land ownership.

The economic freedoms granted after 1978 have, therefore, been limited and only temporary. Peasants have never felt certain if or when the reforms might be reversed. Under the household contract responsibility system, the state did not offer ownership of the land but only 15-year leases. The peasants still had to deliver grain taxes to the state, which operated a purchasing monopoly until very recently. The state continued to directly control agriculture through its grain monopoly, as well as being the sole supplier of seeds and fertilizers, and by fixing prices for many other rural products.

To ensure sufficient food supplies, Deng Xiaoping introduced the one-child policy—in which having one child was promoted as the ideal; while the limit is strictly enforced in urban areas, couples in the countryside are permitted to have two children if the first is a girl. The policy dramatically cut fertility from a national average of nearly six children for every woman to just 1.7 by 2001. No other society in history has reduced fertility so sharply in such a short

After Mao's death in 1976, Deng Xiaoping ended the famine by once again allowing peasants to cultivate private plots.

period, and the results mean that China's population will stop growing and start declining around 2050.

The price paid for this success can be counted in various ways. One is the number of "missing" girls. Sons are preferred for a variety of reasons, including the fact that they are more helpful with farm work, they provide the traditional financial support for parents in their retirement, and daughters cannot inherit. The last national census in 2000 revealed 20 percent more boys than girls below the age of five. In seven inland provinces, with a combined 387 million people, there are between 28 percent and 36 percent more boys than girls in this age group.

"This is huge," said Prof. Judith Banister, a noted U.S. demographer who has pioneered many studies on China's population. "This is the most extreme case on the planet, more extreme than India by a considerable margin."

Girls began disappearing from head counts starting in the early 1980s, and the ratio widened every year until 2000, when the disparity stabilized albeit at a high level. Just how many "missing" girls there are is uncertain, but by 2010 between 40 million and 60 million girls may be "missing"—and, of course, an equal number of bachelors will never find a bride.

What happened to them is still a matter of demographic guesswork. In the mid-1980s, family-planning units across the country were given ultrasound machines to enable the authorities to inspect women suspected of illegally removing their compulsory intrauterine device (IUD). China is the only country in the world to perform this sort of oversight. However, the ultrasound devices also enabled parents to see the sex of the fetus in the fourth or fifth month. If it were a girl, they could then opt for a late-term abortion. The procedure is cheap, as little as 1,000 yuan ($120) for a backstreet abortion and just 30 yuan ($3.60) for an ultrasound scan. A 2002 survey conducted in a central China village revealed that more than 300 of the 820 women had had abortions and more than a third of them admitted they were trying to select their baby's sex.

China carries out some seven million abortions a year, and according to the International Planned Parenthood Federation, more than 70 percent of the aborted fetuses are females. Most of the girls are missing because of these late-term abortions, although Professor Banister believes many others may have been killed or died through neglect and mistreatment in their first three years. "A lot of people in China are determined to have a son," she said. "If they fail to get a boy, most would probably abandon the daughter rather than kill [her]. A lot of children are being abandoned."

Infanticide is hard to prove, but the demographic evidence shows deaths among girls up to age two are far higher than for boys. The phenomenon is also creating a growing number of abandoned children, especially girls. Just how many girls have been abandoned remains a secret, but the orphanages are full of girls, the only boys being those with severe handicaps.

Population policies have also revived the age-old practice of human trafficking—in this case, kidnapping and selling babies. The justice ministry has said that 10,000 babies were rescued during a three-month nationwide crackdown in 2000. Only 1,300 of these children, however, were traced back to their parents. In one case in Henan Province, the police unraveled a sales network operating in five cities in the nearby province of Shaanxi by stationing an officer in the kidnappers' home to take calls and catch other child traffickers. Customers placed orders, mostly for boys, and the gang would then try to meet the request. Baby girls were priced at between 1,000 and 1,400 yuan but healthy baby boys sold at between 5,000 and 8,000 yuan. A renewed campaign against the abduction of children, launched four years ago, has met with some success with the rescue of more than 13,000 children.

China has tried to counter the deep-rooted preference for boys by allowing girls to inherit their father's plot of land and by offering parents who have just a daughter a yearly pension of 800 yuan. Other measures include exempting girls from school fees and granting housing, employment, and welfare privileges to one-daughter families. Still, every year, 3.4 million young rural women try to take their lives, usually by drinking farm pesticides. Suicide is the leading cause of death in the 15- to 34-age bracket in China, the only country in the world where the suicide rate is higher for females than for males.

Some hope has been achieved with the increase of foreign adoptions. Americans adopted about 5,000 Chinese girls every year during the 1990s; in 2003, the number rose to 7,000. Many European countries, especially those with very low birth rates, have been catching up. After the United States, Spain comes next with around 2,100 girls in 2003, followed closely by Canada.

Next to controlling population growth, the government's other top priority was raising food production to feed an extra 15 million new mouths each year—and to meet demand for a richer diet. China has been able to rise to the challenge and extract higher yields because productivity had been so low in the Mao era. Small innovations, such as using plastic sheeting to protect seedlings, have made a big difference. On the other hand, continued success is not guaranteed.

For one thing, the best farmland near the cities is being rapidly lost to urbanization, which means that if China follows the pattern set by Japan, Taiwan, and South Korea, it will become a large food importer. At various times during the 1990s, China imported as much as 17 percent of the world's traded wheat, 25 percent of its fertilizer, and 28 percent of its soybean oil. If per capita–production growth continues to decline, then China could become so heavily dependent on imports that it would need to buy up all the grain now traded in the world market each year. The whole world would be faced with food shortages and high prices.

China has kept food production rising but only through direct intervention, often at the expense of peasant incomes and at the risk of provoking urban anger. When after more than 40 years the state abolished food rationing, including grain rationing, prices jumped, fueling an inflation rate that threatened to spiral out of control. In the 1990s, the government was forced to reintroduce rationing to bring prices down. To do so, it had to outlaw private grain trading. The peasants responded by neglecting to grow enough grain so the state had to jack up its purchasing prices. Domestic prices reached levels well above those on the international market.

The next problem was a surplus. By the mid-1990s, China had piled up such huge grain surpluses that it had nowhere to store it and market prices plummeted again. Equally worrying was the cost of buying and storing this grain. The grain monopoly was draining the state treasury. Between 1992 and 1998, the state ran up losses of 26 billion dollars, and local governments resorted to paying peasants with nearly

On Chinese farms, there is no asset more valuable than children to work the land, and girls are less useful than boys.

worthless IOUs instead of cash. There were riots across the country, and eventually the state had no choice but to announce it would abolish the state grain monopoly.

Relying on Adam Smith's "invisible hand" to balance supply and demand is an enormous gamble. It runs counter to deeply entrenched Chinese political habits and to Maoist principles of self-sufficiency. Yet after many false starts, China is again moving toward a market system for grain, cotton, and other basic essentials. A grain futures exchange has been set up in Zhengzhou, in Henan Province, which helps guarantee producers a fixed sale price and allows private grain dealers to hedge their risk. If this experiment succeeds, it will mark the end of the Chinese

peasants' feudal obligations to the state and weaken the power local officials wield over the peasants.

The next step, still under debate, would be to grant full property rights. A peasant could then sell his plot, or mortgage it to raise capital and later pass it on to his son. When the 15-year leases expired, the peasants were supposed to be granted 30-year leases, but local officials resisted, keen to keep the option of selling land to developers. This situation has been another cause of riots across the country. Peasants have fought pitched battles to protect their land, often against thugs hired by local officials. In 2005, police in Panlong, in Guangdong Province, opened fire, massacring unarmed protesters who did not want their land sold to developers for a special chemical-and-garment industrial zone.

China's 180 million peasant households work an average of just 1.5 acres, holdings too small to justify investing in top-quality seed, irrigation equipment, or mechanized farming. Some 70 percent of the work in fields is now done by women whose husbands are away working in the cities. Only with security of tenure can farmers be expected to make long-term investments and acquire enough land to build commercial farms. To meet its growing needs and compensate for the loss of prime land in places like the Chang Jiang (Yangtze) and Zhu (Pearl) River Deltas, China will have to encourage agricultural investment and raise output from second-grade farmland.

China also will have to create more capital- and technology-intensive industry with more professional farmers, a shift that also requires a social revolution. If farm labor becomes more automatic, then 200 million or even 300 million people will have to find other jobs or move to the cities. China's urbanization rate has risen sharply to 39 percent, although this rate is still less than that in Britain in the 1850s and well below the average of 50 percent in developing countries and 70 to 80 percent in rich countries.

Part of the urbanization growth since 1980 has simply been the result of reversing Mao's rustication of 70 million urbanites; the other part reflects the temporary presence of migrant workers who are not really treated as urban residents. The real migration has yet to begin.

Worried about the country's ability to supply cities with enough food, Chinese leaders have discouraged the expansion of large cities and

Peasants are needed as migrant workers in the cities, but they cannot afford city living and are not allowed to settle.

limited migration to small market towns, like Fengyang, with fewer than 200,000 inhabitants. Even with Beijing or Shanghai, the emphasis has been on developing smaller satellite cities around them.

Fengyang has doubled in size in the past 15 years and is now full of bustling shops and markets, but it offers little else. It serves a rural hinterland where residents are still too poor to demand many services. Nearly everyone in the countryside grows their own daily food and just comes into town to buy clothes or luxuries for the New Year holidays. Until rural residents have more cash to spend, Fengyang, and many places like it, can't grow.

The Great Leap Forward is now officially recorded as an "economic mistake" but nothing more. It is not clear whether the party's intentions have changed much since those days. In a way, what is now happening in China may not seem so different from the 1950s. As during those times, the Communist Party envisions a future in which the peasants will one day move out of their homes into large high-rise blocks and work in large, mechanized, factory-style farms. Industrial growth depends on the crude transfer of wealth from the countryside to the cities. Once more, tens of millions of peasants have been drafted into the cities to work temporarily on a vast and ambitious crash industrialization scheme. The scheme is again being made possible by paying the peasants very low wages or sometimes not paying them at all.

Beijing continues to spend taxes to subsidize the expansion of the state sector, especially the heavy industries like steel and coal. Instead of Soviet experts building factories and transferring technology, this time China is relying on overseas investors. Admittedly, this time Chinese factories are not turning out useless lumps of metal but are in fact assembling high-quality products in high demand around the world—and there is plenty to eat.

Yet the nature of the relationship between the party and the peasants has not changed very much. As a revolutionary party, the Chinese Communists have always relied on coercion, and the enthusiasm for intrusive social engineering remained undiminished by the huge catastrophe of the Great Leap Forward. The peasants are not allowed to form their own political parties or any other kind of organization where they would be able to fight for their interests.

They continue to want to own their land, to govern themselves free from the arbitrary rule of despotic local officials, and to revive their traditional customs and religious beliefs. Instead, the party organizes campaigns to eradicate the revival of local religious practices and prevent the resurgence of local customs. As long as local cadres still have the final say on how land should be used, and could at anytime take away a peasant's plot and give him another, few dare to organize any opposition.

This system has also spawned a corrosive corruption since there is nothing to protect the peasant against land seizure by officials. Any official could take the land and sell it for development of, say, an industrial zone at a vast profit. The value of the land seized in the last decade has been estimated at several hundred billion dollars, and by 2003 there were some 40 million landless peasants.

Of all the issues between party and peasant, however, the one-child policy has probably been the most explosive. The party has had to resort to brutal campaigns, inspections, forced abortions, sterilization, and harsh punitive fines to uphold the policy. Peasants who resist have their homes torn down and their goods confiscated, and in some cases find themselves imprisoned or tortured.

The *hukou* system, which imposes strict limits on Chinese citizens wanting to change their permanent place of residence, has provoked anger as well. The system has been rigidly enforced to prevent peasants from leaving their villages without permission. A new source of grievance was the introduction of compulsory six-year education (later extended to nine years) in the late 1980s. Nearly 90 percent of this education spending has come from local government coffers and local officials could only implement the law by levying fresh taxes, a new and painful burden, on peasants who live in a largely subsistence economy.

As the post-1979 reforms saw local public finances completely decentralized, local officials began to behave like cruel landlords, which in a sense they had become. They introduced more than a hundred different kinds of taxes and fees for everything from building a new road to killing a pig. In 1996 alone, local governments collected 116 billion yuan (14.5 billion dollars) in illegal fees. In some parts of the country-side, officials resorted to the age-old practice of tax-farming, whereby an

official would spend his term milking a locality of taxes and then move on to his next post. Some of them even sold their position to the highest bidder.

Peasants quickly realized they were being squeezed for taxes and that the government was offering no public services in return. The education budget, for example, is devoted to a minority of the urban population. It is prohibitively expensive for most rural parents to put their children through secondary education because school fees for a year start at over 1,000 yuan. UNESCO statistics, therefore, rank China 119th out of 130 countries in terms of its per capita spending on education.

China ranks equally poorly on health spending, even though its barefoot doctors and rural health clinics had once been held up as a model by the World Health Organization. By the 1990s, the local clinics were bankrupt and heavily in debt. Only 20 percent of the state health budget went to rural areas, and peasants had to pay for all health care out of their own pockets. As only one in ten farmers had access to public or cooperative medical care, the hospitals refused to treat anyone who could not put down a large deposit up front.

Medical bills became the leading cause of poverty, especially in rural China, as families went deep into debt to pay hospital bills. Many patients had to leave the hospital halfway through their treatment when they ran out of money. The quality of medical care is poor and often fraudulent. China has been faced with a great shortage of qualified doctors, nurses, and, incidentally, teachers, because few were trained during the ten years of the Cultural Revolution when universities were shut down. Rural health centers and doctors now rely heavily on drug sales, and to boost their incomes they even try to sell unneeded medicine or fake medicine.

To curb the tide of anger at this growing litany of social injustices, local officials were empowered to mete out savage and rudimentary justice in anticrime campaigns. In the infamous 1983 "Strike Hard" crackdown on major crime, Deng Xiaoping had more than 10,000 people executed in one year at public sentencing rallies. The crime crackdown became increasingly used as a tool to tackle growing crime resulting from social and economic changes. In the 1980s, Chinese—nearly always peasants—were executed for the theft or embezzlement of goods worth as little as 30,000 yuan or, under current exchange rates, just $3,614. There are 68 crimes for which the death penalty can be imposed, the highest such figure in any country in the world, many of which are nonviolent crimes. In 2005, China still accounted for 97 percent of the executions carried out in the world.

In 1979 Deng revived the ancient imperial system of *shangfang*, which allowed people with grievances from the Mao era to deliver petitions and seek restitution for the injustices that occurred during the Cultural Revolution. Thousands of people swarmed around Beijing's Yongdingmen Station every day to deliver handwritten letters to a special office opened to deal with the complaints. The peasants had no recourse either to the police nor to the courts. Little or nothing is spent on the justice system in rural China; funds are concentrated on guaranteeing public order in the big cities, where lies the most dangerous threat to political stability.

As of 2004, the government's Office of Petitions was receiving more than ten million individual petitions each year. Most complaints are never resolved or the letters are forwarded directly to the desk of the officials responsible for the dispute. Just two out of every thousand cases are brought to a conclusion.

As people found it easier and easier to travel within the country, tens of thousands started to descend on Beijing in the hopes of lobbying top officials when they gathered to hold a congress or some other party

Even the rudimentary health care available to rural peasants is generally beyond their means to afford.

meetings. Large numbers of police have to be mobilized to detain the petitioners and send them back home.

Political reformers put forward a hopeful solution in the late 1980s. The party passed a law in 1987 establishing village elections, hoping this representation would provide a safety valve for peasant grievances, but the initiative faltered after the Tiananmen Square massacre. The village leaders may have been directly elected, but in the end they had no real power to challenge appointed party officials. Experiments for elections at the township or county level were tried but stopped when the party realized its monopoly on power would quickly vanish because the peasants would not vote for the party's preferred candidate. The failure of both the petition system and the experiments in democracy, naturally, gave the peasants few alternatives but to resort to direct and violent protests.

Although the authorities could stamp out these small local brush fires and prevent them from spreading too quickly, it was not always possible to isolate urban China from the ills of the peasantry. The neglect of public health soon began to show up in an alarming way with a series of health scares. By 2001, the rural neonatal and infant mortality rates were 2.3 times higher than those in urban areas. China has the second highest number of people in the world suffering from tuberculosis, after India, with the disease killing 130,000 Chinese every year.

China became known as the breeding ground for new and often dangerous viruses. It was swept by global epidemics like AIDS; diseases that jumped from animals, like bird flu; and completely new strains of viruses, such as the disease called Severe Acute Respiratory Syndrome (SARS), which the central government tried to hide or deny until it threatened the stability of the urban economy and spread overseas.

In Henan Province, the entire adult population of villages began to die from HIV complications in the early 1990s after peasants were infected while selling blood illegally. By the end of 2005, China said it had 650,000 people living with HIV/AIDS. The U.S. Central Intelligence Agency has projected that China might have between 10 million and 20 million HIV cases by 2012.

Rural China faces an AIDS crisis due to a lack of safeguards in blood banks; this little girl was born HIV-positive.

The government initially paid little attention to the rural health crisis and tried to silence activists who wanted to raise the alarm. Many of the victims were so poor that, even at the best of times, they earned little more than $150 a year. Since a year's supply of the cocktail of drugs needed to control the disease costs about 10,000 dollars, no peasant could afford treatment, and no government authority wanted to accept the responsibility to pay for such costs.

The central government began to react to the rural SARS health crisis only after 2003, when the virus caused alarm all over the world. Panic broke out in Beijing where thousands of people had to be held in isolation, and as people stopped traveling, the whole economy came to a standstill. Across China, officials sealed off villages, patrolled streets, and poked into homes to monitor the health of residents. The government even threatened to arrest and execute people who knowingly spread SARS. The emergency forced a recognition at the highest levels that something long term had to be done.

China may now be poised on the point of a great change. The government wants to speed up what it calls the greatest migration in human history. By 2020 it hopes that 300 million to 500 million people will have moved into the cities. The government has begun to cautiously dismantle the main obstacles to rural migration created by the hukou system. This effort means removing discrimination against peasants by allowing them to obtain employment, send their children to urban schools, and get treatment at urban hospitals and pay the same fees.[3]

In 2005, the central government began putting flesh on a policy of boosting rural incomes with a view to creating a consumer economy. Instead of simply extracting wealth from the countryside, it began to reverse the transfer. One of the first and historic steps has been to abolish the age-old peasant taxes. The first trial started in Fengyang in 2000 with a decision to fix rural taxes at 8.4 percent of a farmer's income and eliminate more than 40 different types of taxes. The Chu family said they were actually receiving a subsidy of 15 yuan per mu instead of paying taxes of 30 yuan per mu. And there are other subsidies for things like planting trees. In Fengyang, both the Chus and Lus said that in the past two years there have been no new protests.

By this time, China's economy has changed so much that rural taxes have fallen to a very minor slice of China's annual tax revenues, which total about 229 billion dollars. Over five years, the benefit for farmers is likely to be equal to more than seven billion dollars.

Beijing has promised to abolish rural school fees and to ensure that all rural children be provided with nine years of free education by 2010, at a cost of 12 billion dollars a year. The central government also said it would pay rural teachers ten billion yuan (1.25 billion dollars) in back pay and will take back responsibility from the individuals for paying teacher's salaries.

China wants to boost spending on rebuilding the rural public health system, and it has started experiments with pilot rural health insurance schemes. The sums are still very modest; one billion yuan (121 million dollars) will go to improving the rural public health infrastructure. Another sum, twice as large, will go to facilities for emergency public health incidents, local disease control centers, and AIDS-prevention programs.

With no local democratic outlets, rural Chinese often try to bring their grievances directly to party officials in Beijing.

In addition, China is seeking to boost farm investment by making more small loans available to farm households through its vast system of 35,000 rural credit cooperatives. During the 1990s, farm loans were frequently squeezed out by loans to rural factories and local governments. The rural credit cooperatives went bankrupt as local governments ran up huge debts (totaling 125 billion dollars). Under a slogan of creating a "more harmonious society," current premier Wen Jiabao promised in 2006 to reform the lower levels of the bureaucracy and to improve rural governance. He also said in a key speech that land acquisition for construction projects would be strictly controlled in the future.

For the first time, households in many rural communities are being offered a micro-lending service. Such loans are small, nearly all under $2,500, and short-term (mostly three to six months). With these, farmers will be able to make modest investments into such things as building new wells, buying livestock or fertilizer, planting orchards, or building greenhouses. Subsidies are available for buying high-quality seeds and new machinery.

The government also began to claim success in a three-year campaign to force employers to make good on some 20 billion dollars in unpaid back wages to migrant workers. The Ministry of Public Security has loosened restrictions to make it easier for peasants to transfer their residency to the cities. Premier Wen further promised to improve migrant workers' labor conditions, including pay, social security, vocational-training opportunities, and their children's education.

The various measures are expected to divert tens of billions of dollars into the rural economy. Rural incomes rose by 16 percent in 2005, the first real rise in more than 20 years, and social tensions have begun to abate. Even so, these changes will take many years to have an impact. They are unlikely to begin to close the still widening gap in living standards between city and country dwellers or to create the common prosperity and harmonious society that the leadership is promising.

The latest batch of reforms still do not tackle basic grievances like land tenure. Promises to give peasants 30-year leases have not been fulfilled. Even if these promises were granted, they would still fall far short of the land ownership that peasants feel is their right. Granting

A woman carries a satellite dish to her home in Jinzhai County, Anhui Province. China is making strides in the self-sufficiency of its rural citizens, and consumer goods are slowly reaching the countryside.

small farmers secure property rights proved to be one of the foundations of the postwar prosperity of Japan, South Korea, and Taiwan. Nor is the government considering, as yet, replacing the one-child policy with more flexible family-planning incentives.

However, the party has begun to address the grievances of peasants. For the first time in generations, the Chinese state has begun to treat the peasants as normal citizens. Transforming the lives of a billion or so Chinese peasants, a number equal to the combined population of the industrialized nations of the world, would not be easy under any circumstances.

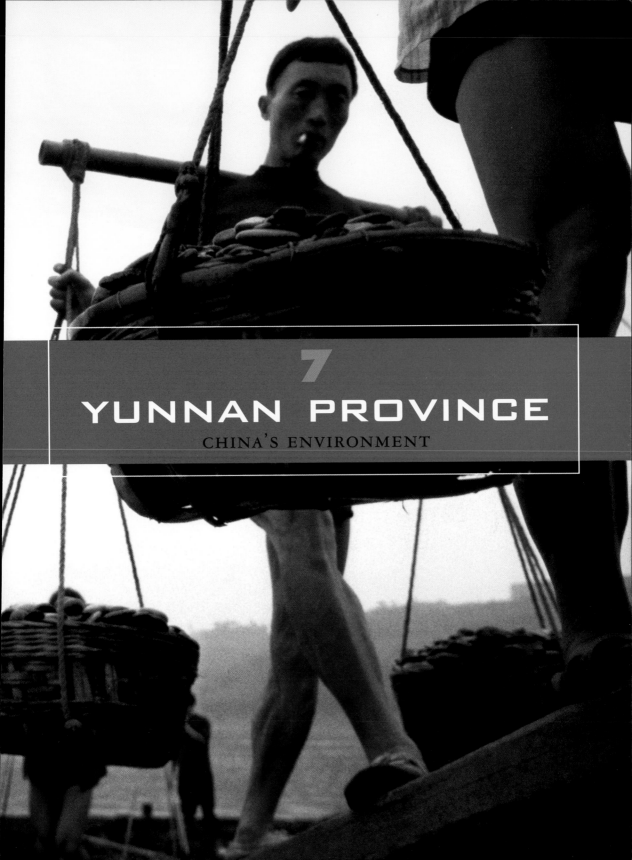

YUNNAN PROVINCE

CHINA'S ENVIRONMENT

CHAPTER SEVEN

Its nose-curling stench hits you even before you see the floating carpet of green algae and dense matting of water hyacinth. Once a beauty spot praised by poets, Dian Chi Lake in Kunming, the capital of subtropical Yunnan Province, shows the cost of China's frantic growth.

"There are fewer fish and they keep getting smaller. They don't taste good, either," complained fisherman Gong Gaoling. When he was growing up in the 1960s, the waters were crystal clear and there were 57 types of fish and shrimp to catch. Now, half of the species have vanished altogether and just six are worth catching.

"When I was young, you could swim in it and see the stones at the bottom," he said. Now the bottom has poisonous sediment of cadmium, arsenic, and lead three feet thick that can be removed only by dredging.

Wherever you go in this beautiful landscape bordering Myanmar (Burma), Thailand, and Vietnam, you find a heartbreaking legacy of environmental mismanagement and the prospect of worse damage to come. Kunming has spent more than two billion dollars on efforts to clean up the lake, but the water is still too toxic to drink and nowhere near meeting the country's minimum quality standards.

The industrial hub of a poor province with 42 million people, Kunming has about 5,000 industrial plants pouring effluent into the lake. For years, time after time, the municipal government ordered the worst polluters to shut down.

Like many of China's lakes and reservoirs, Tianxian Lake in Chongqing Province suffers from uncontrolled pollution.

PREVIOUS PAGES *These baskets of coal being transported in Wushan, in the Three Gorges region, will be used to generate electricity and run industrial plants—in the process creating smoke that befouls China's air.*

"They just pretend. I can hear them when they secretly open again, sometimes at night," Mr. Zhong scoffed. Many factories are still using machinery dating from the 1950s to produce chemical fertilizers or to process tin and phosphorus.

And until the first wastewater plant was built in 1990, Kunming pumped 90 percent of the city's untreated wastewater directly into the lake. About 332 million cubic yards of wastewater are discharged into Dian Chi Lake every year. "Even after treatment you still can't drink this water," admitted Wu Yihui, who manages a plant built in 1996.

Liang Congjie, the founder of Friends of Nature, a Chinese nongovernmental organization (NGO), recalled swimming in Dian Chi Lake as a student in the 1950s and spoke bitterly about the failure to clean it up. "It is awful. They just made a kind of show," he said.

Mr. Liang said the authorities even poured chemicals into the lake to kill the algae and then filtered the water before Kunming staged an international horticultural exposition in 1999. To manipulate scientific data on the lake's effluent levels and to make them match claims of success, local officials would resort to tricks like moving a monitoring station from one end of the lake to the other, cleaner, end to get better readings.

Dian Chi was once one of Asia's biggest freshwater lakes, but over the past 50 years, it has shrunk to a third of its former size and silted up. "Our per capita supply of water is just one ninth of the national average," said Lin Kuang, spokeswoman for Dian Chi Lake Regulatory Commission. "Without the water, we can't grow our economy."

In its search to find drinking water, Kunming has had to build reservoirs and dams on rivers ever farther away. Since the 1980s, the city has relied on water channeled from the Songhua Dam reservoir in the mountains some 50 miles away. Now, as the city prepares to expand, it has also been forced to invest in an even bigger engineering project to divert water from other rivers like the Jinsha (Golden Sands) River, a tributary of the Yangtze River 120 miles to the north.

Major cities across the country are grappling with the same threats as Kunming, and water is only one facet of a crisis that, if unchecked, could overwhelm the whole modernization project. The

Fishermen at Lake Erhai for centuries have used cormorants to catch fish, but there are now fewer and fewer fish.

origins can be traced to a mixture of inherited problems and new ones; in both cases the root causes are political. The environment poses one of the gravest threats to the political stability of the country because it lays bare for all to see the failure of the political system. Environmental protest movements and failures like the accident at the Chernobyl nuclear plant spurred the downfall of the Soviet system in the 1980s. It is remarkable that so far nothing similar has happened in China, because the failures are as painfully evident here. Disputes over pollution is one of the chief reasons for the rapid growth of grassroots protests in China.

In Yunnan, it all started in the early 1950s when the state sent logging companies to fell the forests and settle hundreds of thousands of newcomers. At that time, virgin tropical forest still covered most of the mountains and plains. The great rivers, Chang Jiang (Yangtze),

Mekong, and Salween, rise in the high Himalayan Plateau and flow in parallel through some magnificent steep gorges so remote that Western explorers saw them only at the turn of the last century.

One of the explorers, Joseph Rock, whose travels in the 1930s were published in NATIONAL GEOGRAPHIC, made Yunnan's flora and fauna internationally famous. As Rock revealed, Yunnan is one of the most biologically diverse areas in the world, with half the nation's animal species and a quarter of its plant species. Rock traveled everywhere on foot and horse, and sometimes he had to be carried by porters. The area was still largely untouched by the modern world in 1949.

More than anywhere in China, the blame for what has gone wrong cannot be laid anywhere but on the post-1949 government. In a short few decades, Yunnan's rivers and lakes, including Dian Chi, have all silted up. Even the more recently built dams have begun to suffer as sediment accumulates in the reservoirs and industrial and agricultural effluents poison the water in them.

In this chapter, my journey starts in Kunming at a meeting of environmental NGOs and ends at the Tiger Leaping Gorge (Hutiao Xia), a chasm through which the Golden Sands River hurtles beneath the snowcapped Jade Dragon Snow Mountain (Yulongxue Shan). A dam will soon be built across the gorge and will block all of Yunnan's great rivers, the last pristine rivers left in China. If the dam project moves forward, the rich diversity that Joseph Rock marveled at will be at risk. It is an easy call to make, because one by one all of China's great rivers have already been ruined. The dire state of China's rivers is the most visible evidence of the ecological fallout from policy introduced during the Mao Zedong era that has continued in the market economy era that followed.

The Chinese Communists borrowed from Joseph Stalin the philosophy that "man must conquer nature" rather then live in harmony with it. Stalin's economic policies required rapid electrification. This plan in turn depended on the construction of large-scale hydroelectric schemes and nuclear power stations, which could demonstrate human technological mastery over one of the great forces of nature.

Under Mao, China paid no attention at all to the principles of sustainable growth. In fact, people actually felt proud of pollution

The Yellow River was a particular target of Mao Zedong's drive to tame all of China's wild natural resources. Workers here build the gigantic Sanmenxia Dam in 1958; the dam was later deemed an environmental travesty.

because it was a sign of progress. The more chimneys that belched dirty smoke, the more successful and developed a place could claim to be.

Mao had cultural and historical reasons for his eagerness to conquer China's rivers. China's civilization developed in river valleys, and each dynasty depended on its ability to mobilize large numbers of workers to prevent floods and irrigate fields to ensure prosperity. Mao was especially eager to tame the Huang (Yellow) River, whose frequent devastating floods gave it the name "China's sorrow."

Soviet engineers arrived soon after 1950 and started planning the construction of 46 giant dams across the Yellow River. Before 1949, China had built just 40 small hydropower projects and a handful of larger ones. At the same time, Chinese students were sent to the Soviet Union and began to study hydroelectrical engineering. Among them was the future prime minister Li Peng, who began to harbor the ambition to erect a dam bigger even than any Stalin had ever built—a dam across the Yangtze at the Three Gorges. Nothing less would do to demonstrate China's maturity as a great power.

In 1959, before the first of these Yellow River dams could be completed, Soviet experts withdrew in the midst of a great ideological schism between Moscow and Beijing. The Chinese decided to press on themselves regardless, but the Sanmenxia Dam proved to be a disastrous mistake because, for one thing, the reservoir quickly silted up. Some 300,000 peasants were pushed off their land to make way for the project, and many later died of starvation during the Great Leap Forward. Subsequent engineering efforts did not manage to make it a success, and 40 years on, locals have petitioned the government to dismantle the dam.

Even so, China continued an ambitious dam-building program during the Great Leap Forward. Like latter-day pharaohs, the Communist Party leaders mobilized huge resources and manpower to build dams, big and small. They were built everywhere at a furious pace, often without proper planning or tools, and sometimes in defiance of basic engineering principles. By now China has more dams than any other country in the world. However, some 3,500 of them have already collapsed, and even now nearly 40 percent of the 84,000 existing dams are at risk of collapsing. For decades, China kept hidden news of the world's worst dam disaster, which took place along the Huai River in August 1975: The Shimantan and Banqiao Dams suddenly collapsed and drowned 240,000 people.

China's dams are to blame for other problems, above all for the worsening shortage of water. Some 500 cities are now dangerously short of water. Even by official accounts, 70 percent of rivers and lakes across the country are so polluted they fail to meet government standards, and the water in one in seven major reservoirs is undrinkable.

The rivers and reservoirs around two of the country's most important cities, Beijing and Tianjin, have either run dry or are poisoned. The aquifer below the two cities is being steadily drained; the water table is now 300 feet below the surface and dropping by 10 and sometimes 20 feet a year. This drop means that in Tianjin some 60 percent of the land is plagued by subsidence.

If there is no solution to the water shortage in northern China, 20 million peasants—and perhaps one day many times that number—will be forced to abandon irrigation or will leave marginal farmlands. Some fear that China's water deficit has already become so serious (the shortfall in the north alone is more than ten trillion gallons a year) that the nation's entire prosperity is in jeopardy.

China is spending some 30 billion dollars to ship water all the way from the Yangtze along the South-North Water Diversion Project to keep Beijing and Tianjin going. Tianjin tries to disguise the lack of water in the Hai River, which runs through the center, by importing water diverted from the Yellow River and keeping a stretch of water dammed at either end just for show.

If one takes the night train from Beijing through the Loess Plateau to Taiyuan, the capital of Shaanxi Province, one glimpses factories in steep valleys emitting a grand and yellowish glow amid billowing clouds of black and yellow smoke. In daylight, streams and rivers, where effluents—matte black, ocher red, yellow, and even a Day-Glo green—gently bubble and simmer like a witch's cauldron.

The Fen He River, a tributary of the Yellow River, is now just a ghostly presence in Taiyuan. Not long ago, it was wide and deep enough to carry fleets of barges. Now huge bridges span a bare riverbed along which a trickle of dirty water flows. The Taiyuan Iron and Steel Works, the city's largest employer and polluter, continues to pump out a steady stream of black, foul-smelling water directly into the Fen He. As in Tianjin, a few hundred yards of deep water have been imprisoned and kept for show in the center of the city.

Like Beijing and Tianjin, Taiyuan has been forced to import water from far away. Yet another dam has been flung across the Yellow River at Wanjiazhai in Pianguan County, from where 42.4 billion cubic feet of water is pumped 250 miles to Taiyuan. It is a stupendous engineering feat because the water crosses rough mountainous country; engineers had to bore tunnels longer than the English Channel tunnel and build dozens of aqueducts.

The fate of the Yellow River, which runs through the Loess Plateau, is a warning of what might yet happen to other rivers, even the Yangtze, the third longest in the world. For all but two months of the year, the Yellow River ceases to flow entirely. It is a dry bed 600 miles long.

The Huai River Basin in central China, home to 150 million people, has fared no better than the Yellow River. In all, China built 36 large dams, 150 smaller dams, and 4,000 locks and barrages along its length. Yet instead of preventing disasters or improving the management of water resources, the problems have multiplied. Residents along the Huai River are plagued by constant water shortages. In 1999, for instance, the Huai River Basin suffered a drought for 247 days. Cities and towns had to frantically start digging deeper wells to chase the shrinking aquifers hundreds of feet deeper underground. Even in the best of times, the dams and barrages also trap the pollution released by thousands of factories in the basin, creating undrinkable and toxic reservoirs of water.

The grandiose dam-building mania of the Mao era had other repercussions that became clear in 1998 with deadly floods along the Yangtze River. To create more arable land to grow grain, the Communist Party had drained many of the lakes along the middle Yangtze that held the overflow of the summer floods. Since 1949, two-thirds of the Yangtze lakes have disappeared. The total surface area of the lakes in the middle and lower Yangtze shrank from 6,949 square miles to 2,702 square miles in just 50 years. In China as a whole, wetlands have shrunk by nearly two-thirds since 1949.

The lakes that survived the reclamation drive have silted up. The storage volume of these lakes fell by 282 billion cubic feet. Dongting Lake, the second largest in China, was cut by half and became very shallow as 3.5 billion cubic feet of silt sank to the bottom, raising the bed by 1.4 inches a year.

When the Yangtze flooded more than usual in 1998, there was nowhere for the water to go and the resulting damage cost 36 billion dollars. If the floodwaters had risen a few more inches over the emergency levees, then the loss of life and property would have been far greater. The authorities were poised to dynamite the levees in order to protect the great industrial cities like Wuhan.

Mao's insistence on raising grain production at all costs led to the drainage of lakes and wetlands downstream from Wuhan. It also led to a phenomenon unique to China: a backbreaking effort to terrace steep hillsides after destroying the natural vegetation. Since much of China is mountainous, nowhere more so than Yunnan, the policy accelerated the rate at which silt eroded off steep slopes and filled the rivers. Every year in Yunnan, some 500 people die in floods that wash away not just

Countryside along the Yangtze River in Hubei Province. As hillsides were terraced to raise grain production under Mao's watch, silt eroded off slopes and raised the levels of rivers and lakes, causing massive flooding.

houses but entire sections of roads and railroads. The silt is not just raising the levels of lake beds but of rivers, too, which is forcing the local population to keep raising the levees ever higher each year. By now the Yellow River flows nearly a hundred feet above the surrounding countryside.

As the reservoirs have silted up, the dams have become progressively less useful at controlling floods or even providing reliable flows of electricity. The costs of maintaining the dams and building ever higher flood barriers have often outweighed the economic benefits.

For the Chinese, crowded together in river valleys and relying on limited farmland, the consequences of these errors were felt far more keenly than they were in similar situations in the Soviet Union. The Soviet citizens were, after all, far fewer and scattered over a much bigger territory. The dam-building in China had a direct human cost: To make way for the dam reservoirs, the party forcibly relocated some 16 million people from their farms in fertile valleys and exiled them to poorer lands.

The Mao era had other features that were peculiar to China. Mao's rush to industrialize China led him to order all major cities to invest in heavy industry. The new factories would be built right in the heart of ancient walled cities. Even Beijing, which had no industry to speak of before 1949, soon had 6,000 factories operating inside the old imperial capital. Many were small, but Beijing ended up with its own steel works, machine tool plants, and power plant. But in most cases, little or nothing was invested in water treatment plants. Some 20 billion tons of urban wastewater are currently dumped each year straight into rivers and lakes.

In the countryside, furthermore, the peasants switched from using human waste ("night soil") to fertilize their fields to applying nitrogen and phosphorus fertilizers. This chemically charged runoff promotes the growth of thick films of algae and dense coverings of water hyacinth in rivers, lakes, and canals. Some scientists are convinced there is a direct link between China's water pollution and the country's high rates of hepatitis A, diarrhea, and liver, stomach, and esophageal cancers.

In the end, China did not get a large share of its electricity from the hydropower schemes nor did it invest in a civilian nuclear industry. Instead, it relied on its plentiful supplies of coal for heating and electrical power—so all Chinese cities soon suffered from a suffocating pall of industrial air pollution that was at its worst in winter.

On the World Bank's list of 20 cities with the worst air, 16 are Chinese, and the capital is perhaps the most polluted of all. People in two-thirds of the 338 monitored cities in China breathe air that fails to meet national air-quality goals, which are set well below those established by the World Health Organization. Air pollution related to the burning of coal is believed to kill more than 700,000 people a year. A World Bank report estimates that air pollution costs the Chinese economy 25 billion dollars a year in health expenditure and lost labor productivity. Deaths from respiratory disease increased by more than a quarter in the 1990s.

After 1979, the new government led by Deng Xiaoping began to take environmental issues more seriously and slowly began to admit the scale of the problem. The first environmental legislation was approved, and new bodies were set up to monitor and enforce the legislation. Errors like the Sanmenxia Dam on the Yellow River came to light for the first time. The dam-building program slowed. The government admitted that out of the 16 million people displaced by reservoirs, some 10 million were still living in poverty. A fresh effort was launched to help those relocated find new ways to earn a living and to provide better compensation to new relocatees.

Deng's new agricultural policies helped redress the ecological mistakes of the Mao era. As grain production rose, the state encouraged farmers to abandon the terraces or to grow other crops, including fruit and nut trees, tea bushes, trees, and drought-resistant grasses. Ambitious reforestation programs were unveiled. To combat the growing desertification of northwest China and to protect Beijing from the spring dust storms, it announced plans to build a giant "green great wall"—a belt of a billion newly planted trees.

Then, in the 1990s, the government began addressing the problems of urban China and spending massively on the construction of new housing. It began the complex process of relocating factories from the centers of Shanghai, Beijing, Tianjin, Shenyang, and other major cities. The urban redevelopment allowed a cleanup of polluted waterways like the Suzhou Creek, which runs through Shanghai. As China's leading cities were rebuilt, natural gas pipelines arrived and replaced the old coal-fired heating systems. Households started cooking with clean gas instead of noxious coal briquettes, the cause of so much lung disease.

China's response to the 1998 Yangtze floods was another milestone in Chinese thinking about the environment. The then premier Zhu Rongji ordered a national ban on the logging of old-growth forests, and he commissioned a massive Yangtze-watershed reforestation project. The terraces on all hillsides steeper than 25 degrees were to be replanted with grasses, bushes, and trees. The ten-year program, affecting 200 million peasants, aimed to convert fields back to pasture, forests, lakes, and wetlands.

In particular, Premier Zhu put in motion a plan to re-flood the middle Yangtze wetlands—an integral part of the Asian flyway for swans, herons, storks, ducks, geese, cormorants, egrets, and Siberian white cranes—which has involved moving about 2.5 million people onto higher ground or into small rural townships. The project reversed the Maoist scheme to drain Dongting Lake and called into question the philosophy behind China's water management.

After 1989 Zhu, a Soviet-trained hydropower engineer, pushed through a plan to dam the Yangtze at the Three Gorges against considerable domestic and international opposition. One of the avowed purposes of the dam was to control the dangerous summer floods, although it became clear that even if the dam were completed, it could not prevent floods or even reduce their threat.

Dam opponents put forward many other objections to the scheme, ranging from engineering difficulties to economic cost, and most of all

the difficulty of relocating up to two million residents, many of whom lived in cities and towns along the banks. As the project got under way, it became clear that the original proposal had vastly underestimated the number of urban residents who would have to be rehoused and find new employment, and the amount of farmland available to resettle the farmers who lost their land. It also became clear that the electricity demand forecast was not materializing. In 1998, when China's economy seemed to be contracting during the Asian financial crisis, the project looked like a white elephant in the making.

The trillion-dollar infrastructure-spending program launched in response to the Asian financial crisis and the foreign investment that flooded into after China joined the World Trade Organization in 2001 saved the Three Gorges Dam. Energy demand shot up, far ahead of even the most optimistic predictions. China's accelerating growth has justified the need for hydroelectric schemes as the best way to diversify away from coal.

China sits on massive reserves of coal, which accounts for 75 percent of its energy output. Since 1998 China has doubled its coal production to 1.9 billion tons, mining almost twice as much coal as the United States, the world's second largest coal producer. If China's economy keeps roaring along, it will overtake the United States as the world's largest source of greenhouse gases within a decade, contributing mightily to acid rain and global warming. China has surpassed the United States as the world's largest emitter of sulfur dioxide, and about 30 percent of China's total land area, and more than 60 percent of cities in southern China, are damaged by acid rain. In 2004, acid rain was estimated to cost China more than 110 billion yuan (13.4 billion dollars) a year.

Chinese coal is cheap to buy, but the human cost is high. Officially, China has three million coal miners, who mostly work in 580 big state mines. But in reality, China probably has around 6.6 million miners. The rest work in 70,000 mines run by villages and local governments in which equipment and working conditions are extremely primitive. Most of these miners are local peasants who earn low wages and whose lives are worth little to their employers. As a result, about 6,000 die in Chinese mines every year, a death rate that

The Three Gorges Dam, a Communist Party dream since the 1950s, will disrupt countless lives and flood scenic valleys.

is a hundred times the rate in the United States or Australia. China, which produces a third of the world's coal, accounts for 80 percent of the mining industry's fatalities. In addition, some 600,000 miners suffer from pneumoconiosis, a number that grows by 70,000 a year. Some experts estimate that perhaps the real death toll from mining, if the deaths from lung diseases are included, is about 20,000 lives a year.

Before 1998, Chinese economic planners had been trying to close these small mines, suspend new dam projects, and shelve an ambitious nuclear power plan. A surplus of electricity, plus the disastrous Yangtze floods, had opened a window to pursue more environmentally friendly policies. Yet this window soon closed as economic growth raced ahead and the price of oil and other commodities rose higher and higher on world markets. Between 1998 and 2006, the price of a barrel of oil went from $14 to more than $70. As China became the world's second largest oil importer after the United States, its energy policies had to be drastically revised.

The drive to close small and inefficient coal mines stopped, and every part of China began a frantic effort to build new coal-fired power stations to keep up with the demand. As most coal is shipped by rail, the railways and harbors quickly jammed up, leading to coal shortages. Across the country, 500 new coal-burning power stations were under construction in 2005, and planners now estimate that over the next 30 years half the world's new power capacity will be built in China.

Hydropower engineers took all the dam projects they could find off the shelves and began a new drive to start building new dams in every possible site. They could now safely argue that hydropower is cheaper, safer, and more ecologically sound than coal or anything else. As most of the untapped rivers lie in the west of China—areas like the mountains of Yunnan—China has also begun to invest in a new nationwide electricity grid to transport electricity to the east coast. It is also starting to establish a market for electricity that allows different suppliers to compete on price.

China ranks second globally in installed electricity capacity (338 gigawatts in 2000), but its use of electricity is just 38 percent of the world's average. When you consider that China has 1.3 billion people—more than four times the population of the United States—the implications of the country's gallop toward a Western-style consumer society are sobering. If per capita energy use were to reach the world average, China will have to add the generating capacity of Canada every four years. And even if the lower predictions of per capita energy use are realized, then China is likely to add an extra 200 or 300 million gigawatts before 2050 when the population will peak.

China is rapidly trying to exploit its natural gas reserves and is building a network of pipelines to serve the growing urban population. By 2030, natural gas could account for 8 percent of China's energy needs. Over time, China's cities should enjoy cleaner air as natural gas, instead of coal, is used for heating and power generation.

The Three Gorges Dam will not control the Yangtze's flooding problem when completed by 2009, but it may reduce China's reliance on coal.

China is beginning to ship liquefied natural gas from Australia, Indonesia, and Iran. Also planned are pipelines to bring natural gas from Siberia and Kazakhstan.

There are, in addition, ambitious plans to build a range of nuclear power stations. A handful of plants were built with French help in the 1990s, but China's energy shortages could mean a bonanza for the whole nuclear power industry.

So far, China's search to secure supplies of oil is affecting the rest of the world. China's biggest domestic oil fields in Daqing in the Northeast and the Shengli oil fields in the Yellow River Valley have now peaked. China is tapping new oil and gas fields in Xinjiang Province and offshore in the Bay of Bohai and the South China Sea. It is already in dispute with Japan and Vietnam over the rights to exploit underwater fields farther offshore. It is also competing with Japan to buy Siberian oil, going toe to toe with India to stake out oil fields in Angola and Nigeria, and challenging the United States for access from its traditional suppliers like Saudi Arabia and Venezuela.

Worried by China's hunger for energy, Washington blocked an attempt by Beijing to buy Unocal, a major U.S. oil company. Washington has also become alarmed by China's willingness to make deals with rogue regimes such as Sudan, Myanmar, and Iran that are sitting on untapped reserves. The United Nations has accused Sudan of genocide in the Darfur region, but China remains the largest investor in Sudan, where it has built a pipeline.

China is challenging the global order not only with its search for oil and gas but also with its hunger for minerals, iron ore, copper, aluminum, uranium, and natural resources such as timber, fish, and soybeans. Its needs are so great that if it is not already the largest buyer and consumer, it soon could be. At the very least, its needs are going to shape the environment of its neighbors and economic partners, big and small. The 1998 decision by Premier Zhu Rongji to stop the commercial logging of the remaining domestic forests had immediate repercussions for neighboring Myanmar, where Chinese logging companies arrived to cut down virgin teak forests, and for Indonesia, where the last rain forests are being felled to supply the Chinese market. When President George W. Bush decided against joining the Kyoto

As China becomes wealthier, millions of cars will join those already on the road in Beijing, shown here, and elsewhere, greatly increasing oil consumption and air pollution.

Treaty on global warming, he argued that it would not work if China did not join and control its emissions.

In 2003 China added 1.4 million cars to the 7 million on its burgeoning network of roads, one for every hundred people. If, like Americans, every second Chinese had a car, the country would have 600 million—almost equal to the world's total cur-

rent car population. Such forecasts naturally beg the question of whether China's economic growth is sustainable. Or, to put it another way, is the world going to run out of finite resources like oil before China gets rich? And will China begin exporting its environmental problems to the rest of the world before it improves its own environmental record?

For example, the dams it plans to build along the Mekong and Salween Rivers in Yunnan Province have raised alarm in Southeast Asia and generated protests by environmental groups who fear that they will endanger the ecology of downstream countries. China has plans for a cascade of 13 dams on the Salween River, which after it leaves China runs through Myanmar before eventually forming the border with neighboring Thailand. Nine of these are in the Three Parallel Rivers National Park, which UNESCO designated as a World Heritage site in 2003. China is building dozens of dams on the Mekong and on Yangtze tributaries such as the Golden Sands River. It plans to double hydropower-generating capacity to more than 120 gigawatts by 2010 and to keep building more dams for the following 20 years.

Some of these dams are being built primarily to trap silt and protect existing dams. One of these is the Xiaolangdi Dam built across the

Yellow River. Another is the 722-foot-high Xiluodu Dam across the Golden Sands River. The latter is designed to trap a third of the silt that would otherwise fill up the Three Gorges Dam reservoir and imperil the value of that gigantic investment.

If one looks at the sad fate of the Yellow River, the Huai River, and nearly every other river in China, its neighbors have good reason to be worried. Tens of millions in Myanmar, Thailand, Laos, Cambodia, and Vietnam depend on rivers shared with China for their livelihood.

Efforts to manage the effect of a 50-year-long drought in northern China have not been a success. Most of the trees planted in the green great wall died from want of attention, and the frequency and severity of spring dust storms have increased. The dust is being blown across Korea, Japan, and even as far as the United States. Northern China's water shortages keep worsening, and the solution of shipping water from the Yangtze to supply Beijing can only be a stopgap measure.

The central government in Beijing is calling for more balanced economic development and has even proposed establishing a "green index" by which to measure it. The current premier, Wen Jiabao, has said he wants to see more scientific development, and senior officials are now being judged on their ability to achieve environmental targets.

"We are paying more attention to the transformation of the mode of growth, resource conservation, environmental protection, and, more importantly, the improvement of the lives of the people," said China's top leader Hu Jintao in April 2006. The same month, Premier Wen presided over a two-day environment conference in which he admitted that 8 of the 20 environmental goals set in the tenth five-year plan have not been met, including the limits on the discharges of sulfur dioxide, carbon dioxide, and industrial waste and improvements in wastewater treatment.

The new mood came on the heels of a major industrial chemical spill on the Songhua River in Heilongjiang Province bordering Russia, which forced the resignation of the State Environmental Protection Agency. After an accident in November 2005, a plant owned by the Jilin Petrochemical Corporation released a hundred tons of benzene and other toxic chemicals into the Songhua River, creating a 70-mile slick.

At first Jilin denied the river had been polluted, saying the explosion had produced only carbon dioxide and water, and the company had treated any dangerous effluent. Next the authorities hid the threat to the drinking supplies of cities along the river. When the water supply in Harbin was shut down, residents were told that the works were temporarily closed for maintenance.

The truth could no longer be disguised when the toxic spill approached the border with Russia. In the face of Russian indignation, the domestic media began to loudly denounce the behavior of Harbin authorities. In the next month, the media reported a spate of similar toxic spills into rivers around China.

The story followed a pattern that has become familiar in China. In 1994 the government had announced an effort to clean up the Huai River after a tide of pollution killed off the fish and sickened thousands of people. The State Environmental Protection Agency issued new regulations and a plan to build 52 water treatment plants and close down more than 60,000 small industrial enterprises.

By 2001, the *People's Daily* was claiming victory. It boasted that the government had achieved what had taken other countries 20 years to do, crediting the success to mobilizing the masses. It claimed that the river now met standards set by the State Council, meaning it was at least "grade three" quality—good enough for industrial use but not for drinking.

It took courage for a whistle-blower like Su Kaisheng, a professor at the Huainan Industrial College and vice chairman of Anhui's People's Political Consultative Conference, to challenge this optimistic verdict. As he told the *Worker's Daily,* the river quality was actually grade five—so polluted it is judged too dangerous even to be used to water crops.

He wrote: "To meet the State Council's targets, some provinces gave false figures and made false reports to the central government. As a matter of fact, the pollution has not changed much, although some of the smaller factories have been ordered to halt production." Only 6 of the 52 water treatment plants had ever been built.

China's first environmental law was passed in 1979, and the country continues to produce a slew of environmental laws and regulations.

The top leaders in Beijing seem sincere when they say that environmental protection is a priority. So what has gone wrong?

One problem is that inspectors lack teeth. The factories polluting Dian Chi Lake are fined, but the highest fine ever levied was $8,500. Many find it cheaper to pay up than to install water treatment equipment. As Xu Kezhu, who teaches law at Beijing's Political Science and Law University, told me, "It's just not easy to put the laws into practice. Our legal system is far from perfect."

The economic reforms encouraged an explosive growth of factories and mines run by local and village enterprises and by private entrepreneurs, and they paid taxes, which filled the coffers of local governments.

The fiscal decentralization after 1979 meant that if these enterprises did not produce profits, then local officials, teachers, law officers, and many others could not draw their salaries.

Many of the most polluting industries, including tanning, dyeing, papermaking, and mining, are also the most competitive where margins are cut to the bone. To generate the electrical power needed to expand the economy and to create jobs, many local administrations did not wait for the state to build new dams or power stations but set about building their own small coal-fired power stations, which used the cheapest—and dirtiest—equipment. In a sense, the reforms have simply moved the pollution out of the cities into the countryside.

China's high growth rates are based on an extraordinary degree of wastefulness. China takes six times more electricity to make a ton of steel than Japan and three times as much as most European countries. The country's 500,000 industrial boilers that produce most domestic heating are a third less efficient than those in the rest of the world. If the real environmental costs are deducted, then one ought to cut China's economic growth rates by between 2 and 5 percent.

All this pollution brings local government into conflict not only with the edicts from Beijing but also with local residents. Wherever you go in China, you find communities of farmers or residents caught up in bitter battles with local officials over pollution that is destroying their health or their livelihood. A young woman named Miss Xu helps run the Center for Legal Assistance to Pollution Victims in Beijing, staffed by students from the Political Science and Law University, which in 1999 opened a hotline to help the victims of such conflicts. It was immediately flooded with up to 300 calls a day.

One case involved thousands of peasants in a county a few hours south of Beijing. The local government depended on the profits from a handful of factories that make zinc-electroplated metal coils. The factories had pumped its toxic wastewater underground using a technology that has been outlawed outside of China. The poisonous wastewaters seeped into the aquifers from which the villagers drew water to drink and water their crops. Children began to die and many villagers had serious skin diseases. The peasants went to the press and tried to take the local officials to court—a court that was controlled by the local

As areas of the countryside become contaminated with industrial pollution condoned in the name of progress, the beauty of the landscape—such as that found outside Lijiang in Yunnan Province—will be lost forever.

party. When I visited the villagers, they were frightened to go public and pleaded with me to keep their names out of the press, lest the local police arrest them for forming an illegal organization.

At present, it is strictly forbidden to unite workers, peasants, religious believers, or students in any organization that challenges the authority of the Communist Party. In theory, the village democracy law, passed in the 1980s, allows the peasants to elect their own representatives on village councils. So far these are the only direct elections regularly permitted in China, although there have been experiments in a handful of places where township leaders have been directly elected.

China is also deliberating new legislation to define the activities of nongovernmental organizations. China already has thousands of NGOs. However, the membership and influence of environmental groups like the Green Earth Volunteers and the Friends of Nature are closely circumscribed. Many depend indirectly on foreign funding from sources such as the Ford Foundation. Others are so closely supervised by the Communist Party that they are dubbed GONGOs, government-organized nongovernmental organizations.

One successful Yunnan NGO, Green Plateau, was started by a couple from Beijing, Xi Zhinong, a wildlife photographer, and his wife, Shi Lihong, a journalist. Mr. Xi visited the forests around the 20,000-foot Meili Shan glacier to take the first pictures of a rare species, the golden snub-nosed monkey. A few thousand monkeys still roam across these mountains, but state logging companies were about to move in and destroy the last natural forests left in the region. The couple raised the alarm, and the distant government in Beijing gave way to an intensive lobbying effort and put the forests under protection.

In Kunming, I attended the fourth NGO forum, at which Sierra Club visitors, among others, gave lectures advising how best to organize a media campaign. It is hard to digest the lessons of foreign counterparts, however, because the Communist Party's tolerance of NGO activities is unpredictable.

The host of the Kunming meeting was Prof. Yu Xiaogang, who had founded an NGO called Green Watershed to protect the Three Parallel Rivers' biodiversity. At that moment, the party had become alarmed by the "color revolutions"—nonviolent resistance against governments in which protesters adopted a specific color as their symbol—that had recently toppled post-Soviet leaders in Ukraine, Georgia, and Kyrgyzstan. Professor Yu decided it was wiser not to speak at the meeting when the police advised him to lie low.

It is easy to understand why the party fears environmental groups could become the nucleus of a popular uprising. Environmentalists can easily rally more than 100,000 people to oppose big projects like a new dam because in China so many people have to be relocated. At the Kunming meeting, there was much talk of the movement to oppose the Tiger Leaping Gorge Dam planned for the Golden Sands River. Some eight Chinese NGOs had signed a petition against that dam and were actively helping the 100,000 people who live near the Tiger Leaping Gorge to organize themselves. And they were gearing up to stop other local projects, including the first dam on the Salween River.

The movement against the dam at Tiger Leaping Gorge—which is so narrow a tiger once supposedly leapt across it—had become a test case for environmental activism, so I decided to trek along the ten-mile gorge and interview some of the local activists. At Shigu, an ancient trading town on the first bend of the Golden Sands River, I found Yang Xueqing, one of the local leaders. His home was in a cluster of old tiled houses with upturned roofs that will be submerged if the dam is built. A tubby brown bear of a man who makes a living from farming and trading, Mr. Yang believed there was still a good chance to stop the dam or at least to influence the decision-making process. He was busy studying China's legal system to see how best to do so.

China had just recently adopted a law requiring major projects to pass an environment impact assessment (EIA). To show it had teeth, the State Environmental Protection Agency had just ordered the halt of 30 large projects, including 26 hydropower plants, that had failed to submit proper EIAs.

The law gave environmentalists a new weapon because, for the first time, it included the requirement to hold public consultations. Local residents would have a voice and could influence other government agencies such as the Forestry Commission, the National Minorities Commission, and the Land Administration Agency, which would also get involved.

"We want people to hear our voice," Mr. Yang said, taking out a copy of the village election law to see what it permitted. "We also want to speak to the media."

His opponents can wield great political influence, but Mr. Yang thought he could mobilize public opinion on his side. The dam is to be built by China's biggest independent power producer, the Huaneng Group, run by Li Xiaopeng, whose father, former prime minister Li Peng, oversaw the massacre on Tiananmen Square and pushed through the Three Gorges Dam project despite a surprising show of public opposition. Big dams are profitable. Power companies can recoup their investment in ten years and local governments in this region can triple tax receipts once the dam is built. Yet the dams almost without exception impoverish those who lose their land and homes.

Mr. Yang had gone to investigate the fate of the 60,000 moved to make way for the Manwan Dam on the Mekong River in another part of Yunnan, some 200 miles to the south. "People were given new land, but it is quite inferior to what they had. So they are now worse off," he said. Mr. Yang and his neighbors will be forced to relocate high up the steep, pine-clad slopes of rugged 17,000-foot peaks if the Tiger Leaping Gorge Dam is built. "And there was lots of corruption," he continued. "The local government gave the resettlement money to a businessman who invested in a marketplace, hotels, and restaurants. Then his company went bust, so all the money was lost."

It was a familiar story. With the Three Gorges, the government originally promised each family a lump sum of between 20,000 and 30,000 yuan, a lifetime's savings in an area where annual cash earnings total not much more than 1,000 yuan. Then Beijing switched to a new policy called "development resettlement." Now two-thirds of the money was to go directly to local officials, and households would get the rest. The local governments were supposed to invest the funds in new infrastructure and factories. Since no accounts were ever made public, though, the peasants suspected that most of the money was embezzled. The judiciary prosecuted some cases, but the policy led to unrest all over the region.

A group of senior men from Gaoyang Township who represented 100,000 peasants whose land was about to be submerged by the Three Gorges reservoir made a collective protest. After a series of riots in which some peasants stormed local party offices, the representatives traveled to Beijing. They brought documents and petitions signed with thumbprints to bolster their claims that they had been cheated. It did the peasants and the representatives little good. Within six months, the men who came to Beijing had been thrown in jail and were serving three-year jail sentences for sedition.

I told Yang Xueqing this story, but he was not put off. The Tiger Leaping Gorge is almost as famous as the Three Gorges, and he treated me to a long exposition on the region's unique history and culture. "This is a happy place where all kinds of nationalities live in harmony. No one wants to leave this beautiful place," Mr. Yang said. The gorge is home to diverse peoples, including the Lisu, Naxi, Han, Tibetan, Yi,

The plan to dam the Tiger Leaping Gorge by 2008 has caused controversy with environmentalists, while 100,000 residents, including outspoken critic Xie Liangping, a farmer from Wuzhu village, will have to be displaced.

and Zhang. The Naxi have a matrilineal society led by shamans who developed their own hieroglyphic writing system that dates back to the 14th century. The neighboring county of Zhongdian tried to cash in on this by renaming itself Shangri-La (Xiang Ge Li La in Pinyin) and asserting that it is where the 1933 novel *Lost Horizon* was set.

Joseph Rock's reports of Yunnan's diversity of cultures and plants may indeed have inspired English writer James Hilton to write his fantasy about a party of Westerners lost after a plane crash who discover a hidden valley of happy Tibetans led by a high lama. As I followed the trail along Tiger Leaping Gorge through the bamboo groves and pine forests high above the rushing waters, I thought a lot about this book. I gazed up at spectacular walls of gray rock topped by white glaciers. Even so, it is warm here year-round as my guide, Xiao Chun, a 17-year-old Naxi, told me. It was December, but the birdsong, the smell from the profusion of wild and exotic flowers, and the colors of the butterflies were magical.

We spent the night at the Halfway Guesthouse run by a jolly Naxi matriarch, Feng De Wang. In the morning we sat in the kitchen tucking into a breakfast of banana pancakes and steamed bread, and she talked about the racial harmony that reigned here. "Her father is Lisu and her mother is Zhang," she said pointing to her staff in turn. "His father is Tibetan and his mother is Naxi. In some households there are seven nationalities."

In *Lost Horizon,* the high lama is a European who 200 years earlier had stumbled into Shangri-La and decided to make it a sanctuary and repository for all the values that he foresaw would be destroyed in the civilized world outside by a coming catastrophe.

As development encroaches China's far reaches, the age-old traditions of its minority groups—here, the Khampas—are at risk.

Much is being lost and sacrificed as China rushes headlong into modernization, but even here people wanted to embrace change. Mrs. Feng was promoting her guesthouse on an Internet webpage. Xiao Chun guided me along the trail while flicking open his mobile phone to chat with friends. The locals appreciated a new road that ran along the side of the gorge, where there was even a parking lot for buses carrying tourists who had started to arrive. I didn't get the feeling that even in Tiger Leaping Gorge the locals wanted to live cut off in a backward Shangri-La, however beautiful and harmonious.

Yet China's insistent push to modernization was giving people little choice or opportunity to question, delay, or preserve what was most valuable. Even when UNESCO designated the Three Parallel Rivers National Park a World Heritage site in 2003, the Yunnan authorities deliberately excluded Tiger Leaping Gorge from the park when its boundaries were negotiated. Those battling to preserve ancient towns, traditional buildings, and diverse cultures and customs face an uneven struggle. The promises to create a more evenly balanced development remain just that—promises. It is a loss that one day everyone will regret.

8
CHINA AND THE WORLD

CHAPTER EIGHT

I n a small workshop in Mandalay, Myanmar, not far from the gilded palace of Burma's last king, the sales girl delicately lifted a leaf of beaten gold between her fingers and opened her mouth. Then she closed it again.

"You don't believe me?" She teased and laughed. "The Chinese people put it on birthday cakes, on dumplings, on all kinds of food. They say a little gold is good for your health."

Miss Moe, who works in her family's King Galon Gold Leaf workshop where craftsmen hammer gold into ever thinner pieces to gild wooden statues of the Buddha, was explaining how it had other uses. Then she placed the gold onto her tongue, left it there a moment to show me, and then swallowed.

"See, you can eat gold," she said. "I have eaten two pieces today. And I am fine."

Mandalay, Myanmar's second city, is home to one of the country's largest Chinese communities, whose fortunes along with China's are on the rise.

I had come here to look at China's impact on the world at large. All too often English-speaking readers think solely in terms of how the West is changing China, or the reverse, but China's rise, as I discovered, is a global phenomenon. Its trade with Myanmar is worth 1.5 billion dollars, an insignificant part of China's global trade, which hit 1.3 trillion dollars in 2005. But for all that, Myanmar is an instructive place to contemplate

Chinese immigrants in countries throughout the world—here in Singapore—often reside in separate Chinatowns and maintain many of their traditional ways.

PREVIOUS PAGES *Taiwan fiercely proclaims its autonomy, but it is the ascendant People's Republic that has the world's attention today.*

how in the 21st century China is affecting all countries, no matter how small and isolated.

Southeast Asia is home to 40 million overseas Chinese, and in Mandalay's Chinese temples, shops, and restaurants, I met the descendants of refugees who had fled the Japanese invasion. Many came from Guangdong and Yunnan Provinces and arrived during the 1930s and 1940s with nothing.

As in most cities across Southeast Asia, the Chinese are found in a distinct Chinatown in the commercial center. In Mandalay, the community of about 100,000 makes up a tenth of the population. Above the doorways, Chinese-character signs announce the presence of temples, schools, churches, and *hui guan,* or guild houses. They mostly own gold-, gemstone-, and timber-trading businesses and live in big villas scattered around the outskirts. In a country with a failing currency like Myanmar, their gold shops are crowded with customers counting out huge piles of cash and converting it into gold. Although they lost nearly everything when the country's ruler, Gen. U Ne Win, nationalized their businesses in 1962, they are now prospering again, partly thanks to opportunities created by China's boom.

In the capital Rangoon, I was told that a million Chinese have migrated into Mandalay and other towns close to the Chinese border, buying up fake citizen documents, taking over farmland, cutting down trees, and flooding the markets with Chinese goods. The story has become widespread. In the book on globalization *World on Fire,* by American writer Amy Hua, I read:

> Mandalay's central business district is now filled with Chinese signs and Chinese music pouring out of Chinese shops. Burmese-made products have been almost entirely displaced by cheaper Chinese imports. Chinese restaurants serving grilled meat and fish overflow with loud Mandarin-speakers. 'To go to Mandalay,' snaps a character in a local cartoon strip, 'you need to master Chinese conversation.'

When I visited Mandalay in 2006, it took me several days to come across anyone speaking Mandarin, and there was no visible presence of Chinese from the People's Republic of China (PRC). A few traders came to buy gemstones and jade, and there were a few company representatives and some tourists, but nothing more foreboding.

Mandalay, with a population of nearly one million, lacks any kind of nightlife apart from three karaoke bars. While there are certainly plenty of Chinese goods on sale in the market, there were just as many goods available from South Korea or Japan.

Yet China is the only big country backing the military junta that rules Myanmar, supplying it with aid and arms. Western countries have isolated Myanmar and banned all investment after the military ignored the results of the 1990 elections and arrested the winner, 1991 Nobel Peace Prize winner Aung San Suu Kyi. Poor and stagnant Myanmar is now run by a group of generals who make up the State Peace and Development Council. Most days the English-language newspaper, the *New Light of Myanmar*, carries a front page highlighting the activities of Senior Gen. Than Shwe.

Visiting Myanmar makes one wonder whether the PRC might now resemble a giant Myanmar if the West had imposed the same blanket sanctions in 1989 after the Chinese military had crushed the pro-democracy protests. Instead, Western countries chose to engage China and have poured investment into the country, hoping to influence a gradual political change. So far, the result has not been democracy, but China is much freer and more prosperous than it was.

Myanmar is also a good example of how China's new economic might is beginning to challenge the club of Western nations and Japan, which have set all the rules in the global economy since World War II. China's newfound influence as a world power is, however, not as new as it seems.

Gemstones and other precious commodities are the stock in trade of many Chinese expatriate entrepreneurs.

The history of Burma (which became Myanmar in 1989) shows how China's power has waxed and waned, with huge repercussions for its neighbors. Going back 800 years to the Yuan dynasty, the Mongols invaded Burma three times. There were two more invasions in the following Ming dynasty, and in the Qing dynasty the Burmese kings sent regular tributary missions to Beijing with gifts of elephants.

The Qing emperors exercised their sway over most nations in Indochina as well as Korea, Tibet, Mongolia, and inner Asia. The arrival of Western nations changed all that. The Portuguese, Dutch, French, and British established trading outposts and colonies. The British ousted the last Burmese king in the late 19th century and established their military headquarters on the grounds of Mandalay's beautiful moated palace. They were followed in 1941 by the Japanese with their effort to unite all Asian nations under the auspices of the Greater East Asian Co-Prosperity Sphere. The palace was destroyed in fighting between the Japanese and British-led armies and has since been restored.

One of the goals of China's modernization project has been to restore all the territories lost to the Japanese and others during the decline of the Qing dynasty and to rebuild China as a great power, without equal in the world.

For the Burmese, the Koreans, the Vietnamese, and others, the modern nation-building task has been to free themselves of all colonial powers, including the Chinese. It is no wonder that many Burmese now find the prospect of becoming a Chinese client state yet again somewhat alarming and tend to view the Burmese-Chinese population as a potential "fifth column." Burmese Chinese did in fact play a leading role in the now defunct Burmese Communist Party (BCP), which was controlled and armed by Beijing and several times came close to winning power.

Under Mao Zedong, China exerted a vast influence, ideological and military, over the whole region. The Chinese Communists sent a million troops to Korea, half a million to Vietnam. Chinese troops occupied Tibet, invaded India, and attacked the Soviet Union in border skirmishes that almost led to full-scale war in 1969. The Chinese Communists financed and trained long-running insurgencies in Malaysia, Burma, Cambodia, Laos, Thailand, Indonesia, and the Philippines. Southeast Asia was close to becoming for China what Eastern Europe was for the Soviet Union.

China wanted to establish itself as the leader of a world revolution and take over the leadership of the communist movement from Moscow. Toward this goal, it also trained and armed protagonists in Third World wars in places as distant as Angola, Mozambique, South Africa, Zimbabwe, Somalia, Ethiopia, Lebanon, Palestine, Sri Lanka, and Peru. There are still Maoist armies fighting on in Nepal, India, Peru, and the Philippines.

Some of the Chinese who settled in Southeast Asia over the centuries as traders joined the Chinese Communist Party (CCP) or played leading roles in establishing national Communist parties. Many were poor, especially those who in the last decades of the Qing dynasty had left their homes in search of work. The British brought them to Burma to grow rice and to what is now Malaysia to work on the rubber plantations. The Chinese were known to work harder than the indigenous peoples. Although they arrived as penniless indentured laborers, they could latch onto earlier Chinese trading and shipping networks. They opened shops and small trading businesses, and prosperous and distinct Chinatowns expanded in Saigon, Bangkok, Singapore, and every corner of Southeast Asia. Rangoon has half a million ethnic Chinese, about a tenth of the capital's population.

The divided loyalties of these overseas communities mattered less when the common enemy was Japan. The Japanese first invaded and conquered China and then Southeast Asia, and the ethnic Chinese played a leading role in the resistance. After Mao came to power, many Chinese communities split, some remaining loyal to the Nationalists (KMT) but others siding with Mao and aggressively spreading his thoughts in their host countries. In British Malaya, ethnic Chinese gathered in the jungle and led a dogged Maoist insurgency that was only narrowly defeated.

In Burma and elsewhere, the Chinese grew to dominate trade in many key commodities, including rice, and resentment sometimes exploded in anti-Chinese riots. Chinese shops and warehouses were ransacked, Chinese homes burned down. All too often, the fate of the ethnic Chinese populations suffered when the Communist threat became too acute. Politicians stoked simmering resentment against the Chinese and turned it to their advantage. In Indonesia in 1965, Gen. Haji Mohammed Suharto instigated riots that destroyed the powerful Chinese-led Indonesian Communist Party.

The Burmese Communist Party was nurtured during World War II when it took part in the anti-Japanese resistance and obtained arms and training. BCP guerrillas fought with the British and helped defeat the Japanese. In 1948, after Burma became independent, the BCP retreated to the mountains of central Burma from where it waged a fierce guerrilla war. In the 1950s, the party commanded as many as 30,000 followers. As Burma was beset by ethnic conflicts, as much as two-thirds of the country was outside of Rangoon's control. There were still tens of thousands of KMT forces who were forced over the border when Chiang Kai-shek lost power. Some KMT soldiers settled in the country and helped create the opium business in the Golden Triangle. Most left Burma in 1958 and crossed into Thailand.

After the 1960 Sino-Soviet split, the BCP sided with the Chinese and took its orders from the CCP's International Liaison Office in Beijing, which in turn acted according to the shifts in power between Mao and his critics. The BCP's prospects of winning power were very promising in the '60s. Most young Burmese students were ardent Maoists. After Gen. Ne

Win seized power in 1962 and introduced the "Burmese Way of Socialism," he antagonized the Chinese by confiscating and nationalizing the property of the ethnic Chinese. When peace talks with the BCP broke down, the new government imprisoned thousands of left-wing activists.

Burmese students who were already avid Maoists joined the fight in the jungle. The interests of the Chinese community in Burma and the BCP now became completely entwined. The country became steadily poorer and more isolated under Ne Win's misrule. In 1967, he encouraged or tolerated a wave of anti-Chinese riots, blaming the Chinese for rice shortages.

The BCP, however, failed to make any headway because it had become caught up in China's Cultural Revolution. The BCP split into two factions: the red flag and the white flag factions. Burma had its own militant Red Guards, who killed hundreds of older "right-wing" BCP members and expelled many others. The BCP lost public support among the majority Burmese population. Some BCP members made their way to the Burmese border with Yunnan Province, where China set up a Burmese government-in-exile.

The anti-Chinese riots gave China an excuse to intervene. In 1968, it invaded Burma in an undeclared war that was little noticed because it took place during the Tet Offensive in Vietnam. In support of the BCP, Beijing sent 30,000 heavily armed troops who rapidly occupied swaths of the country and established a separate state with its own currency and stamps. Ne Win, however, managed to break BCP control over central Burma and began negotiating deals with Beijing.

The early 1970s marked the high tide of Chinese influence across the region. One country after another fell like dominoes into the hands of Communist revolutionaries. The United States was in full retreat. In the biggest setback, the Vietnamese Communist Party defeated South Vietnam with China's considerable help. The BCP troops, which contained many professional Chinese soldiers, were still launching offensives even in 1975.

Yet Mao's revolution was a failure, and for China its successes, like those in Vietnam, were Pyrrhic. After uniting the country, the Vietnamese switched their allegiance to Moscow and turned on the Chinese communities, forcing most of them to flee as refugees.

These Chinese merchants saw the British take over Burma in 1886; China now seeks to regain its lost influence there.

Deng Xiaoping responded by punishing Vietnam in a brief border war in 1979, which caused 80,000 casualties, mostly on the Chinese side. The dispute with China, Vietnam's enemy in many periods of its history, led to a war in Cambodia where China had finally succeeded in creating its first full-fledged client state. Vietnam invaded and overthrew Pol Pot's government, forcing his Khmer Rouge back into the jungle. China continued to support Pol Pot until his death, but China's ties with the Khmer Rouge were always more of a burden than an asset.

China had poured aid worth several billions of dollars to support just tiny Cambodia. The cost of subsidizing other clients like North Korea and Albania, and funding large-scale insurgencies like that of the Burmese, put an enormous strain on the impoverished giant.

Soon after Mao's death in 1976, Deng Xiaoping began a long retreat from all these commitments. The effort to spearhead a communist revolution across the globe ended, and Beijing stopped propagating Mao Zedong thought at home and abroad. Deng badly needed the help of the United States and other Western nations for his economic reforms and so he called on the help of the overseas Chinese communities scattered across Southeast Asia. Beijing no longer wanted to antagonize the leaders of countries like Indonesia, Malaysia, and Thailand, where some of the region's wealthiest Chinese families were living. It took some 20 years for Beijing to fully normalize these relations.

After 1979, Deng told all those who came to see him that China needed to take a low profile in international affairs. China needed a peaceful international environment to concentrate on putting its domestic house in order. What China wanted from the outside world was access to markets, investment, and technology. The insurgencies in these countries, however, did not disappear overnight. The Burmese Communist Party, for instance, still commanded a heavily armed and numerous force when in 1988 Burma erupted in a massive revolt against the aged Ne Win. "If the Burmese Communist Party had entered the country then, they would have been welcomed with open arms by the population," veteran Burmese journalist Ludu Sein Win told me.

With 30,000 troops at their call, the BCP could have seized power and kept it, but China hesitated. It would send the wrong signal to the outside world, and, besides, the CCP was in the midst of its own power struggle between those for and against political reform. The result was a damaging rift within the party that allowed the 1989 pro-democracy protests to gather strength.

In China, the crisis ended when the military sent tanks into Beijing. In Burma, Ne Win retired and the country held its first democratic elections. In the end, the result was the same. Although Aung San Suu Kyi, the daughter of the hero of Burma's independence movement, Gen. U Aung San, and her supporters triumphed in the elections, the Burmese military crushed the democratic movement, killing and arresting thousands of students and imprisoning Aung San Suu Kyi.

Yet the differences between the paths taken since then by China and Burma are revealing. In China, the military soon began to withdraw from politics and is today entirely absent from the day-to-day running of the country. In Burma, the opposite happened: The generals hold every important position and control everything. Equally telling, China moved to reassure its neighbors of its intentions. In 1993, China cut off its aid for the BCP, and the government-in-exile dissolved. After more than half a century, the Chinese Communists abandoned their effort to take over Burma.

China generally chose to cultivate a low profile in international affairs during the 1980s and 1990s, although it did cause alarm when it asserted sovereignty over the Spratly Islands, a cluster of atolls in the South China Sea.

In the past few years, China's power has been increasingly revealed through its economic importance. So as China stopped trying to overthrow the Burmese government with military aid and training, it became the Burmese government's most important ally. Since 1990, China has provided Myanmar's military dictators with more than two billion dollars' worth of arms and ammunition. In return it imports teak and gems, wants to import oil and gas along a pipeline, and has a market for large quantities of light industrial goods.

China's backing for Rangoon may be just a matter of simple economic expediency, but it raises bigger questions: As its economy grows, will China wield its newfound influence wisely?

For the Burmese opposition, China's willingness to help an unpopular government stay in power is considered shortsighted because it will encourage latent anti-Chinese sentiment. "Now if you ask any Burmese, they will say the biggest enemy is China. It is the only government to give full support to the military regime. If this goes on, we will become a client state of China," said Ludu Sein Win. "Many Burmese look to the Americans to save them."

China's rise has created huge new opportunities for the overseas Chinese business community and their adopted countries, lifting their status and visibility. Yet there is a flip side to this new status. Across the region, Chinese businessmen have worked very closely with military regimes and become immensely rich in the process. Their companies control many key business sectors. In Myanmar, ethnic Chinese play a large role in certain businesses such as timber exports, gemstones, jade, and

especially the smuggling of opium and other narcotics. Burmese Chinese, like the infamous opium warlord Lo Hsing Han, who owns the Asia World conglomerate, control the largest private companies.

When public anger erupts against corrupt and unpopular governments, Chinese communities can be targeted. There were violent anti-Chinese riots in Indonesia when the Suharto regime fell in 1998. Even in Thailand, where the ethnic Chinese have integrated better than elsewhere, taking on Thai names and adapting to the customs of their host country, anti-Chinese sentiment remains a big issue. After one leading ethnic Chinese businessmen, Thaksin Shinawatra, was elected prime minister, his huge family business interests became a political liability. Malaysia introduced laws restricting the economic and political influence of the large ethnic Chinese minority's power after violent anti-Chinese riots in 1969.

It is possible that China could seek to use its growing power to challenge U.S. power, as Ludu Sein Win suggests, and force smaller countries to choose between the two. Since the Allied victory in the Pacific in 1945, the CCP has been the chief obstacle to Washington's goal of spreading democracy across Asia. The two sides have fought three major wars and many proxy conflicts: America "lost China" when the CCP defeated the U.S.-backed KMT in the Chinese civil war. The CCP fought the United States to a standstill in Korea in the early 1950s and then helped defeat the U.S. in Vietnam. In addition, China armed and trained U.S. enemies in every other corner of the region.

More recently, America's engagement with China and the opening of its market to Chinese exports is based on the belief that closer contacts will help change China and bring about democracy. However, this detente started as an unlikely military alliance. President Richard Nixon originally came to China in 1972 to forge a partnership against the Soviet Union, which was developing an increasingly threatening naval presence in the Pacific.

After Moscow's defeat in the Cold War, the need for this common front vanished. The Maoist revolution was in retreat, and the cause of democracy made rapid gains in the region. A series of "people power" uprisings took place in South Korea, the Philippines, Taiwan, Indonesia, Thailand, Hong Kong—and, of course, Myanmar and China itself.

Since 1989, Myanmar has become more and more militarized, while in China military dominance has largely vanished.

Democratic governments were elected in Latin America and Eastern Europe. In Central Asia and the Caucasus, most of the newly independent states also held elections, although most remained under the sway of former Communist dictators.

America's global influence soon seemed unchallenged. In addition to these gains, its victory in the first Gulf War against Iraq demonstrated the overwhelming superiority of the U.S. military compared to any other possible rival.

When Bill Clinton took the presidential office in 1992, he accused his predecessor, President George H. W. Bush, of "coddling" the dictators in Beijing. At first President Clinton put forward tough conditions that China had to accept if it wanted to normalize relations and gain entry into the World Trade Organization (WTO, then known as the General Agreement on Tariffs and Trade). Each year Congress voted on whether to renew China's most favored nation (MFN) trading status. This meant that each year Beijing was faced with the threat of trade sanctions.

China refused to accept Clinton's conditions. Furthermore, it demonstrated that if the United States wished a confrontation, Beijing could make a great deal of trouble if it chose to do so by, for instance, helping rogue states in the Middle East acquire weapons of mass destruction. Washington's attempts to impose its will on China were also frustrated by Japan, Germany, and other important nations that scrambled to win business as China began importing their products on a large scale. Economic growth soared to 14 percent after 1992, when Deng unleashed a new wave of reforms, and leaders like Germany's Helmut Kohl led large delegations of businessmen to China and left announcing deals worth billions of dollars. Even France, which had reacted with fierce moral outrage at the Tiananmen massacre and switched its attentions to Taiwan, was forced to make an awkward about-face to get back into Beijing's graces. The U.S. became isolated, and the first Clinton China policy collapsed.

In his second term, President Clinton swung toward more or less unconditional engagement. His administration concentrated on negotiating a deal on China's entry into the WTO, which detailed a road map for China's economic reforms. Step by step, China would open up its markets to the outside world. In exchange, the United States ended the annual ritual of the MFN debate. When China formally joined the WTO

Presidents Bill Clinton and Jiang Zemin sparred publicly over human rights and the Tiananmen Square massacre at a joint news conference in 1997, but U.S.– Chinese diplomacy continues.

in 2001, it no longer needed to fear the threat of economic sanctions by its important trading partners.

The WTO deal, like the WTO treaty, sets the rules for trade but has no social provisions. It does not oblige China to undertake any social reforms, like permitting free trade unions. Chinese leaders reassured visitors like Clinton that their goal remained democracy, but they made few concrete commitments.

China's assurances that it would adopt international standards in all areas, including human rights, were accepted at face value. China's change would take place at its own pace, but as it adapted to the world economy, it would gradually integrate itself into the rules-based international system. In fact, Western countries granted China exemptions in many matters partly due to its huge size and importance, and partly because pressure on, say, human rights was felt to be counterproductive.

As China's economy took off again in another boom after 1998, the United States was confronted by a new problem. As companies from all over the world flocked to China to open up factories and take advantage of the cheap nonunionized labor, China's global clout began to grow faster than anyone might have predicted. Companies could not only make China part of their global manufacturing operations but also tap a huge and still undeveloped market. China's own domestic demand for manufactured goods and for raw materials has soared.

China's appetite quickly became so large that it seemed to be driving the world economy. Take the price of oil. It had slumped to $12 a barrel in 1997; six years into China's boom, oil prices topped $70 barrel. In the first years of the new century, China accounted for 21 percent of world copper and aluminum demand, 11 percent of nickel use, 27 percent of steel demand, and 33 percent of iron ore consumption, driving up the profits of multinational mineral companies like Rio Tinto or BHP Billiton. Ever rising Chinese demand for both copper and nickel has led to global shortages. Global copper consumption in the first seven months of 2004 exceeded production by 710,000 tons. "China's rapid growth is sucking up resources and pulling the region's varied economies in its wake," observed Jane Perlez in the *New York Times*.[1] "The effect is unlike anything since the rise of Japanese economic power after World War II."

Countries such as Brazil that never had any historical trading ties with China have been swept along by the impact. Chinese domestic soybean production has doubled since 1995 but its imports have soared 1,000 percent, to the benefit of producers and shippers in Brazil and Argentina. China, which also buys large quantities of iron and other minerals, has emerged from nowhere as Brazil's second biggest trading partner, rivaling the United States.

All across Latin America, China has been buying and investing in minerals, oil, and gas and exporting growing quantities of textiles, shoes, and consumer electronics at prices that even low-wage countries like Mexico struggle to match. In 1975, total trade between China and the region was a mere 200 million dollars, slowly reaching 2.8 billion dollars by 1988. From 1993 to 2003, China–Latin American trade expanded by 600 percent and total trade between the two reached 26.8 million dollars, of which 14.9 billion dollars were Latin American.

All of a sudden, China's influence now seemed to be growing at the expense of the United States. China overtook the United States as South Korea's biggest trade partner, and soon Japan was importing more from China than the United States. Even when the Sudanese government was condemned at the United Nations for tolerating genocidal policies in the Darfur region, China emerged as Sudan's champion. Beijing supplied it with arms and loans and prevented the UN from imposing sanctions. The Chinese state oil company PetroChina is the largest investor in Sudan and has developed several oil fields and built a 930-mile-long pipeline, a refinery, and a port.

For some European leaders, China began to seem an attractive counterweight to the world's only superpower. European Union leaders like

China's growing global interests reach even to the heart of Latin America, investing in this Bolivian tin mine, for example.

Romano Prodi, the Italian socialist politician who was European Commission president, became eager to enter into a strategic relationship with China and pressed to share new technologies like the Galileo global-positioning system and to lift the arms-sales embargo against China. The latter initiative was blocked by Washington only at the last moment.

China's explosive growth has overturned some assumptions and led to new ones about what the future holds. China has been hailed as the new Japan, and some pundits have extrapolated from existing trends and projected them into a future in which China is destined to overtake the United States. Fifteen or even ten years earlier, such notions would have been met with laughter. In the years after 1989, the Central Intelligence Agency assumed that the CCP would fall from power and feared that China would dissolve into many states like the Soviet Union.

Whatever the case, observers have been quick to declare, like

William Rees-Mogg, the former editor of the *Times* of London, "This is the Chinese century." Famous economists announced that before the 21st century is through, China will have overtaken the United States as the largest economy, and hence the greatest power, in the world.[2] When the *Wall Street Journal* asked ten Nobel Prize–winning economists which country in the world had the best policies, most agreed it was China. Joseph E. Stiglitz, for instance, said, "Based upon the overall economic performance, China is obviously the best, and it has also showed excellent economic management abilities during the East Asian financial crises. From the viewpoint to economic growth rate and flexibility, China has been highly impressive."

This sort of enthusiasm caused one commentator in China's *Southern Weekend* newspaper to express puzzlement and even dismay. "The highly complex state of China is not understood by foreigners. Sometimes, even the Chinese do not understand themselves," wrote Zhang Jiehai in "Cool Reflections on China Fever."[3]

As Mr. Zhang went on to point out, most foreigners base their assumptions on short visits to Beijing and Shanghai or take China's statistics far too seriously. In a country where there are no opinion polls, no political opposition, and no elections, China's economic statistics are the only source of information. However, because all information and research are very closely controlled, this sort of data is very easily manipulated. The temptation to do so by a state whose only source of legitimacy is its economic success must be very strong.

How should one then think about the future in China's century? A few points are self-evident. China-watchers have a poor record of getting things right. Thirty-five years ago, China was still deep in the Cultural Revolution and no one could have then foreseen what it would be like today. Trying to predict what China will be like in 2040 seems foolish.

It is also evident that, in theory, a completely open world economy would see the prices of labor, goods, and products reach the same level everywhere. That premise would mean that if China had three or four times as many people as the United States, then its economy would be three or four times as big. And a country where most people work 70 hours a week can quickly catch up with the likes of France or Germany where they work a 35-hour week.

Among the many obvious unknowable factors is how China's political system will develop. Poor government (as well as invasions and wars) is to blame for the fact that China never realized its potential in the 20th century. The past quarter-century of largely peaceful and stable government has made a large difference, but this period must still be considered exceptional rather than the norm. Even so, the political reforms that were hotly debated in the 1980s in the upper ranks of the CCP have been shelved.

As a result, China is making very slow progress toward developing the strong institutions—an independent judiciary, an elected parliament, a free press—that inspire long-term confidence in the prosperity and stability of successful Western countries. China's political and legal system still remains deeply rooted in its Leninist origins, which is one reason why the extent of the change in China can be overestimated. A modern Western political system was always one of the goals of the first reformers. Democracy, along with science, was defined as one of the two essential requirements for making China modern.

So far, the CCP has managed to avoid another major confrontation over this issue. It has crushed the domestic democracy movement. Since it took over Hong Kong, it has also frozen the movement for a directly elected legislature and chief executive in defiance of popular wishes. Since the mid-1990s, Taiwan has been the only part of the Chinese world to become a full-fledged democracy.

Beijing fired warning missiles toward Taiwan and was openly critical of the winning candidate, Lee Teg-hui, when the island held its first direct presidential elections in 1996. Although the threats to invade Taiwan are wrapped in a flag of nationalism—the desire to prevent Taiwan independence—the CCP feels directly threatened by Taiwanese democracy. It calls into question the CCP's own failure to carry out its promises to introduce democracy.

The two issues of democracy and nationalism are closely linked. The CCP regards itself as having inherited the mantle of the last Chinese imperial dynasty and is committed to regaining control over all the territories lost by the Qing dynasty in its sunset years. One of those territories lost to Japan after a naval defeat in 1895 was Taiwan, a Japanese colony for 50 years after the Treaty of Shimonoseki until it became a U.S. protectorate and then was governed by the Nationalists after Chiang Kai-shek retreated there with his army and followers in 1949. For a long time, it was a one-party dictatorship and the KMT was equally committed to a vision of China as a large unified centrally governed state with the same boundaries as the Qing dynasty at its greatest extent.

The Qing dynasty was an aggressive imperialist state that in the lifetime of just one of its emperors, Qianlong, doubled in size. Qianlong's armies conquered vast territories like Xinjiang, where the majority of inhabitants are not Chinese by any definition. The Qing Empire also claimed suzerainty over the Tibetans or Mongols by virtue of feudal professions of personal loyalty to a Manchu emperor. The Manchus themselves were not Chinese, and when the Manchu Empire ceased to exist and China became a republic, those events severed the earlier relationship. After 1911, many areas and provinces of China formed independent states, including Tibet, Mongolia, Yunnan, and Manchuria. Mongolia's independence was even confirmed by a plebiscite held on Joseph Stalin's insistence after 1945.

Therefore, if the Taiwanese are allowed to freely vote on whether or not they belong to the Chinese state, it would call into question the whole basis of the People's Republic of China. A pro-independence candidate, Chen Shui-bian, has twice been elected president of Taiwan, albeit with slim majorities. Both he and his followers would like to hold a plebiscite and declare formal independence but are discouraged from doing so by the threat of a war with the PRC.

As some 60 percent of the territory of the PRC is inhabited by ethnic minorities—and there are 55 minorities, whose numbers total around 100 million—it is only a short step to imagining how China would break apart if it became a democracy. And many Chinese provinces have larger populations than Germany, the biggest state in Europe. Even Hong Kong, with eight million, is large enough to aspire to statehood.

At the same time, by invoking the imperial legacy and holding to a centralized one-party state, the CCP inevitably has to retain many of the institutions of an imperial state. The head of the Communist Party is at once the head of the state and head of the armed forces. He is also something more—a figure uniquely responsible for the well-being of every member of the Chinese race, even those outside the borders of China who are citizens of other states. Chosen in secret by a self-selected

Displaying typical Taiwanese defiance at interference in their affairs by Communist China, a 1996 campaign poster shows Lee Teng-hui defending the island from Chinese missiles during the 1996 "Missile Crisis."

group, he occupies a position, immune from criticism or question, akin to the pope. And like all past Chinese emperors, he rules through an appointed bureaucracy. Senior officials in the hierarchy, like earlier Confucian mandarins, are regularly rotated so as not to build up independent local power bases that could challenge Beijing's authority.

Imagine if China became a democracy and every provincial governor or mayor was directly elected by his or her constituents. They would expect their representatives to be answerable to them, to promote their local interests, and to pass local laws and budgets. In that case China would have to become a federal state like the United States, or a looser union like the European Union, or perhaps a vague association like the British Commonwealth. In the latter, the queen is the nominal head of state of some members, like Australia or Canada, but not others. Such ideas about federalism have been debated by intellectuals on the mainland, but China has not permitted any public debate on the subject to flourish. It is hard to say how popular such ideas could become if they were ever openly discussed.

The state fosters a powerful sense of nationalism and the need to avenge injustices and humiliations inflicted by other countries in the past. In the history taught in schools, China is always presented as a victim, never as an expansive imperial power. Such notions have put down strong roots and may be hard to change. They are very much in the imperial tradition, which held that the emperor of China had no equals in the world and always acted with benevolence toward lesser nations.

The issue of Taiwan is, therefore, more than a territorial dispute but a lightning rod for a whole raft of issues, such as how China views itself and its historical legacy, and the expectations the United States has for China—the most important issue that divides the two countries. U.S. military power protects Taiwan and its democracy. America's engagement with China is intended to spread democracy to China, something that would assure America's own security. For many, Chinese nationalism is all about conquering Taiwan, resisting U.S. interference, and avenging the humiliation inflicted by Japan. Nationalism rather than communism is now the glue that unites China.

As China grows wealthier and rebuilds the strength of its armed forces, it seems intent on directing its growing diplomatic influence toward forcing countries to support its claims on Taiwan, isolating the Dalai Lama, and silencing its domestic critics. It is increasingly rare for any of its neighbors to give a platform or refuge to anyone that Beijing considers its enemy. Key American allies such as Australia and Canada, which now depend on China to buy their exports, are increasingly uncertain whether they would side with United States in a war over Taiwan.

Beijing is now pushing for regional political and economic groupings that it can dominate, for example, a proposed East Asia Free Trade Area that would exclude the United States. It is negotiating with the ten-member Association of Southeast Asian Nations (ASEAN) group for a free trade agreement, and it seems only a matter of time before China surpasses America's trade with Southeast Asia. And China is acquiring influence in ways it never could before: dispersing bilateral aid, offering loans and special access to its market to poorer countries, and joining broad multilateral aid bodies like the Asian Development Bank.

Some believe China wants to create a global bloc like the European Union and fear that, like the Qing dynasty with its tribute system, it will dominate its neighbors politically, economically, and militarily. China is no longer exporting an ideology, like Confucianism or Maoism, but it does exert some "soft power" because its domestic policies are winning admirers around the world.

It must be one of history's little jokes that the last major Communist Party left in power is burying socialism around the world and embracing private capital. To compete on the world market with China's exports, other countries have to abandon restrictive labor practices and discard state ownership of the means of production. China's impact on that other Asian giant, India, has been considerable. Envious of China's growing strength, India has begun opening its economy to foreign investment and freeing up the domestic economy.

Even in sleepy Myanmar, the military government has traded the "Burma road to socialism" for the "Burma road to capitalism." It has begun to sell off state companies, privatize new sectors, and encourage competition in areas like air transport that have been state monopolies.

As its own economy takes off, India has begun to compete with China in a global hunt to secure supplies of energy and other raw materials. Observers worry that there is enough oil or minerals on Earth to

feed China's voracious demand for raw materials. Just before my visit to Myanmar, the Indian president had paid a rare state visit, a sign that India, too, wanted to tap the country's oil, gas, and timber resources. India and China will become strategic competitors in what was, after all, once known as Indochina.

China's seemingly insatiable hunger for natural resources has left almost no corner of the world untouched. The trucks carrying heavy loads of teak logs from Myanmar's virgin forests into Yunnan Province are only part of the story. China's fishing fleet, the world's largest, is accused of overfishing not only the coasts around China but elsewhere, causing tensions with the Philippines, Vietnam, and Japan. A drop in world fishing stocks and a fall in global catches are blamed on China.

The search to secure new mineral sources has led China to plan investments in India, Mongolia, Pakistan, and faraway Chile. In Papua New Guinea, China is planning to invest 650 million dollars to develop a nickel deposit to cope with a worldwide shortfall of nickel supplies. It is the same story with aluminum: By 2005, a total of 40 percent of new demand came from China. Consequently China has announced plans to invest in refineries and bauxite mines in Brazil, Queensland in Australia, Dac Nong in central Vietnam, and India's Gujarat State.

China's demand for steel has boosted the fortunes of the steelmakers across the world. Since the construction boom started in 1998, iron ore prices have tripled as China has overtaken Japan as the world's largest consumer. It has been a windfall for countries like Australia and Canada, which have rushed to open new mines to keep up with demand.

China's biggest impact is on the energy market. Before 1993, China had been self-sufficient in oil and gas, and indeed, had nurtured hopes of becoming a net exporter as it explored fields in the South China Sea. Since then it has accounted for between 20 and 40 percent of new demand.

Even in Africa, China has become the first or second largest buyer of oil from Angola, Gabon, and Sudan and has been negotiating with Algeria, Tunisia, Togo, Benin, and Egypt. In Angola where it once backed the losing side in the long-running civil war, it won a battle to win exploration contracts by offering a two-billion-dollar development loan. Chinese engineers are now busy constructing roads, houses, ports, and bridges in Angola.

China imports most of its oil from the Middle East and, as in Myanmar or Sudan, has been taking advantage of Western sanctions by fostering close relations with Iran, which supplies 13.6 percent of its imports. Iran has an estimated 939-trillion-cubic-foot gas reservoir, the second largest in the world, about half of which is in offshore zones. Iran has signed a 25-year deal to export gas to China that might be worth 100 billion dollars.

China has been busy negotiating to secure equally large deals for gas in Australia, Indonesia, Canada, Kazakhstan, Russia, and even Myanmar. Its search for energy has led to clashes with Vietnam in the South China Sea and a heated dispute with Japan over the ownership of undersea gas fields in the East China Sea.

Much of the imported oil and gas arrives by ship, but China is anxious about its dependence on supplies coming through strategic choke points like the Persian Gulf and the Strait of Malacca. Since China ended

On a state visit to London by Chinese President Hu Jintao in 2005, protesters ensure that China's human rights failings are not forgotten.

its self-imposed isolation, it has tried to open borders and build new roads, railways, and routes by air and sea. It has been busy constructing or planning a network of long-distance oil and gas pipelines. Pipelines from Kazakhstan, Siberia, Pakistan, and Myanmar are on the drawing board that would link to China's own growing domestic network.

On the other hand, Myanmar illustrates why reports of China's influence, even over its poorer neighbors, can be overblown. Chinese aid is far too limited to make any impression on a country with economic needs the size of Myanmar's. China, in addition, may be that country's largest trading partner, but all goods move through just three obscure border towns: Ruili, Jiegao, and Yinjian. They are carried by trucks on one road, the famous Burma Road, which was built during World War II. Construction of a railway linking the two countries that was started in colonial times has still not been completed; it will take another six years before it is operating. Beijing also wants to run a 600-mile, two-billion-dollar pipeline to carry oil from the deepwater port of Sittwe to run along the railway. If the past is an indication, this project will take longer than expected before it is up and running.

Yet it is true that China is set to develop from a regional to a global power. It is busy forging new security relations. In Central Asia, there has been talk of a "New Great Game" as China establishes new ties with newly independent states like Tajikistan, Kyrgyzstan, Kazakhstan, and Uzbekistan. China has been particularly innovative in Central Asia, organizing a joint security system with the "Stans" and holding joint military exercises through the Shanghai Cooperative Organization. Kyrgyzstan's troops were the first-ever foreign troops to be invited to hold maneuvers inside China.

It also means that China's own troubled minority regions such as Xinjiang and Tibet, beset with simmering independence movements, are now being tapped for their much-needed mineral resources. A large-scale migration of ethnic Chinese to Xinjiang has resulted in a Han Chinese population that now exceeds the indigenous population. A new railway has been built over the high mountains to Tibet that will facilitate mass Chinese migration for the first time in history.

The impact of China's entry into the global economy can already be measured: consumer goods have become ever cheaper and commodities ever more expensive. World commodity prices are at historic highs. Can this growth be sustained? China says it can. It plans to eradicate poverty within its borders by 2050, to establish itself as a world power in science, and to lift the average lifespan to 80 years. The "China Modernization Report 2006" drawn up by the country's leading research institute, the Chinese Academy of Sciences, forecasts that China will move from a predominantly agricultural society to a suburban, knowledge-based economy.

If the country can maintain its current 9 percent rate of economic expansion, then the average income will rise to 16,000 dollars. Half the population will own a car and be able to afford overseas travel. By 2050 some 500 million Chinese will move into industrial cities and 80 percent of the population will be urban. China intends to double its research-and-development budget so that by 2020 it will be spending 2.5 percent of its gross domestic product on R&D.

However, even He Chuanqi, who led the Chinese Academy of

China desperately needs oil for its booming industries and is willing to get it from international pariahs such as Iran.

Sciences research team, told local reporters that China's economic situation is a hundred years behind that of the United States and that in his opinion there is only a 6 percent chance of such forecasts coming true. In the past China has often disappointed optimists, just as the fears it has inspired have usually proved overblown. China, for example, has only recently begun to equal the share of world trade it had in the 1930s of around 4 percent.[4]

The official rosy scenario could be derailed by many factors. One is the environment. China has one of the lowest per capita water rates in the world but is already so desperately short of water that it has to ship water from the Chang Jiang (Yangtze River) to supply Beijing and Tianjin. By the time China's population hits 1.5 billion sometime in the middle of the 21st century, for half the population to enjoy living standards equal to America's, China would have to quadruple its water supply and it would have a fleet of passenger cars of 600 million, almost equal to all the cars now in the world.

The rush for profits at all costs has left behind a hefty environmental debt, and this sort of growth is not sustainable. In Southeast Asia, China is accused of exporting its problems by building upstream dams across vital rivers like the Salween and Mekong. After China declared a moratorium on logging in 1998 to protect its own environment, Chinese logging companies moved into northern Myanmar to cut down teak forests.

China's high growth rates often seem created by gains from short-term policies. Within the foreseeable future, China will have rebuilt all its major cities and sold off 50- or 70-year leases for all the urban land. It will be some years before such large-scale construction will be needed or can be financed. High levels of infrastructure spending cannot be sustained for long.

Likewise, China cannot support economic expansion for long if it continues to pay factory workers such low wages. Henry Ford, remember, felt he had to pay his workers enough money so they could afford to buy his Model T cars. The peasant factory workers who are supposed to move permanently to the cities will have to be able to afford urban lifestyles.

Then there are demographics. The legacy of China's state-owned-enterprise problem is that most cities have a declining and aging population. Four retirees will have to be supported by one child, the product of the one-child policies. The largely unsuccessful efforts to rescue the

At Hong Kong Disneyland. In two decades, China has gone from communist introvert to capitalist flagbearer and may indeed be the land of tomorrow.

SOEs have left a legacy of heavy debts and uncovered pension liabilities. Yet despite such problems, it seems improbable that China would reverse its policies and retreat into the past. China's growth is proving to be a largely benevolent phenomenon bringing everyone more benefits than problems. Chinese visitors indulging in gold leaf on their dumplings are vastly preferable to revolutionaries armed with Kalashnikovs and waving little red books.

As I boarded a small prop plane at Mandalay's deserted airport and headed for the crowded bustling city of Kunming, across the border in Yunnan Province, I couldn't help feeling that, unlike Burma, China was fast becoming a more normal and open country where the odds on more successful change are lengthening.

ENDNOTES

CHAPTER 1 Beijing: Where China's Been and Where It's Headed
[1]Y.C. Wang, *Chinese Intellectuals and the West, 1872–1949,* University of North Carolina Press, 1966, pp. 394–95

CHAPTER 4 South of Shanghai: Private Enterprise
[1]"Two face death penalty for billionaire's slaying," *China Daily,* July 24, 2004
[2]OECD Economic Survey: China, 2005
[3]"Yangtze River Delta Fuels Pollution Crisis," *China Daily,* September 26, 2005
[4]"Inconspicuous Consumption," *The Economist,* December 20, 2005

CHAPTER 5 Pearl River Delta: Rural Migration
[1]Keizai Nihon, "Toyota Opts For Robots As Japan Rejects Unskilled Immigrants," *Nihon Keizai Shimbun,* January 6, 2005
[2]Thomas Fuller, "The Workplace: Where Growth Roars Job Creation Whimpers," *International Herald Tribune,* February 1, 2006
[3]Joseph Kahn, "Ruse in Toyland: Chinese Workers' Hidden Woe," *New York Times,* December 7, 2003

CHAPTER 6 Central China: Agricultural Life and the Initiation of Reforms
[1]Li Zijing, "A Half Million Peasants Plunge Into Rebellion in Four Provinces," *Hong Kong Cheng Ming,* No. 238, August 1, 1997, pp. 19–21
[2]"A Chronology of Unrest: March 2003–December 2004," China Rights Forum, No. 1, 2005
[3]"China Encourages Mass Urban Migration," *People's Daily,* November 28, 2003

CHAPTER 8 China and the World
[1]Jane Perlez, "Across Asia, Beijing's Star Is in Ascendance," *New York Times,* August 28, 2004
[2]William Rees-Mogg, "This is the Chinese Century," *The Times,* January 3, 2005
[3]Zhang Jiehai, "Cool Reflections on China Fever," *Southern Weekend,* January 11, 2006
[4]Jia Hepeng, "Researchers Predict Modernization Progress," *China Daily,* February 9, 2006

INDEX

Illustrations are indicated by **boldface**. If illustrations are included within a page span, the entire span is **boldface**.

ILLUSTRATIONS CREDITS

Cover Photograph; Yang Liu/CORBIS

4-5, Alessandro Digaetano/Polaris; 6, David Butow/Redux Pictures; 12-13, Michael Wold/laif/Redux Pictures; 14, Nina Berman/Redux Pictures; 17, Photo by Time Life Pictures/Mansell/Time Life Pictures/Getty Images; 20, Photo by Dmitri Kessel/Time and Life Pictures/Getty Images; 25, Keystone/Getty Images; 28, Elliot Erwitt/Magnum Photos; 31, Rene Burri/Magnum Photos; 34, Mark Henley/Panos Pictures; 37, Mark Henley/Panos Pictures; 38-39, David Butow/Redux Pictures; 40, David Butow/Redux Pictures; 43, Henri Cartier-Bresson/Magnum Photos; 47, Garofalo Marco/Grazia Neri/Polaris; 51, Bettmann/CORBIS; 52, Alessandro Digaetano/Polaris; 54, Photo by China Photos/Getty Images; 57, Riccardo Venturi/Contrasto/Redux Pictures; 60, Nina Berman/Redux Pictures; 63, Mark Leong/Redux Pictures; 65, Photo by China Photos/Getty Images YH20050620001; 66-67, Adrian Bradshaw; 68, Chien-Min Chung/Polaris; 70, W. Robert Moore/NGS Image Collection; 73, Jim Brandenburg/NGS Image Collection; 75, Bruce Dale/NGS

Image Collection; 78, Adrian Bradshaw; 83, Photo by China Photos/Getty Images; 87, Reza/NGS Image Colllection; 91, Alessandro Digaetano/Polaris; 94, Alessandro Digaetano/Polaris; 97, Mark Henley/Panos Pictures; 98-99, Alessandro Digaetano/Polaris; 100, Michael Wolf/laif/Redux Pictures; 103, Reinhard Krause/Reuters/CORBIS; 105, Claro Cortes IV/Reuters/CORBIS; 108, James L. Stanfield/NGS Image Collection; 111, AP/Wide World Photos/Eugene Hoshiko; 114, AP/Wide World Photos/Eugene Hoshiko; 118, Mark Leong/Redux Pictures; 121, Qilai Shen/Panos Pictures; 124, Justin Guariglia/CORBIS; 127, David Butow/Redux Pictures; 128-129, Gilles Sabrie/CORBIS; 130, Michael S. Yamashita/NGS Image Collection; 133, Mark Leong/Redux Pictures; 134, CHINA PHOTOS/Reuters/CORBIS 137, Ian Berry/Magnum Photos; 139, David Butow/Redux Pictures; 142, Michael Wolf/laif/Redux Pictures; 145, Photo by China Photos/Getty Images; 148, John Stanmeyer/VII; 152, CHINA PHOTOS/Reuters/CORBIS; 156, CHINA PHOTOS/Reuters/CORBIS; 159, Alex Majoli/Magnum Photos; 160-161, David Butow/Redux Pictures; 162, Enzo and Paolo Ragazzini/CORBIS; 165, David

Butow/Redux Pictures; 168, Michael Wolf/laif/Redux Pictures; 173, George Silk/Time and Life Pictures/Getty Images; 176, Raymond Gehman/NGS Image Collection; 181, Gilles Sabrie/CORBIS; 182, Andrew Holbrooke/CORBIS; 186, CHINA NEWSPHOTO/Reuters/CORBIS; 188, Qilai Shen/Panos Pictures 190, Mark Ralston/AFP/Getty Images; 193, Wilson Chu/Reuters/CORBIS; 194-195, George Steinmetz/CORBIS; 196, Doug Kanter/Polaris, 199, Jeremy Horner/Panos; 201, Henri Cartier-Bresson/Magnum Photos; 205, Alessandro Digaetano/Polaris; 208, Peter van Agtmael/Polaris; 210, Chris Stowers/Panos; 213, Mark Henley/Panos; 216, Chien-Min Chung/Polaris 220, Tatlow/laif/Redux; 223, Katharina Hesse/Freelance; 224-225, Simon Kwong/Reuters/CORBIS; 226, Steven Raymer/NGS Image Collection; 229, Mark Henley/Panos Pictures; 232, Hulton-Deutsch Collection/CORBIS; 236, Steve McCurry/NGS Image Collection; 239, AP/Wide World Photos/J. Scott Applewhite; 241, AP/Wide World Photos/Dado Galdieri; 245, Chris Stowers/Panos Pictures; 248, Stephen Hird/Reuters/CORBIS; 250, AP/Wide World Photos/Greg Baker; 253, AP/Wide World Photos/Kin Cheung.

DRAGON RISING

by Jasper Becker

Published by the National Geographic Society

John M. Fahey, Jr., *President and Chief Executive Officer*
Gilbert M. Grosvenor, *Chairman of the Board*
Nina D. Hoffman, *Executive Vice President;*
President, Books Publishing Group

Prepared by the Book Division

Kevin Mulroy, *Senior Vice President and Publisher*
Leah Bendavid-Val, *Director of Photography Publishing*
and Illustrations
Marianne R. Koszorus, *Director of Design*

Barbara Brownell Grogan, *Executive Editor*
Elizabeth Newhouse, *Director of Travel Publishing*
Carl Mehler, *Director of Maps*

Staff for this book

Barbara A. Noe, *Editor*
Jane Menyawi, *Illustrations Editor*
Kay Kobor Hankins, *Designer*
Nicholas P. Rosenbach, *Map Editor*
Gregory Ugiansky, *Map Production*
Lise Sajewski, *Editorial Consultant*
Mike Horenstein, *Production Manager*
Abby Lepold, *Illustrations Specialist*
Robert Swanson, *Indexer*
Jack Brostrom, Amy Jones, Cinda Rose, *Contributors*

Rebecca Hinds, *Managing Editor*
Gary Colbert, *Production Director*

Manufacturing and Quality Management

Christopher A. Liedel, *Chief Financial Officer*
Phillip L. Schlosser, *Vice President*
John T. Dunn, *Technical Director*
Vincent P. Ryan, *Director*
Chris Brown, *Director*
Maryclare Tracy, *Manager*

Founded in 1888, the National Geographic Society is one of the largest nonprofit scientific and educational organizations in the world. It reaches more than 285 million people worldwide each month through its official journal, NATIONAL GEOGRAPHIC, and its four other magazines; the National Geographic Channel; television documentaries; radio programs; films; books; videos and DVDs; maps; and interactive media. National Geographic has funded more than 8,000 scientific research projects and supports an education program combating geographic illiteracy.

For more information, please call
1-800-NGS LINE (647-5463)
or write to the following address:

National Geographic Society
1145 17th Street N.W.
Washington, D.C. 20036-4688 U.S.A.

Log on to nationalgeographic.com;
AOL Keyword: NatGeo.

For information about special discounts for bulk purchases, please contact National Geographic Books Special Sales:
ngspecsales@ngs.org

Library of Congress Cataloging-in-Publication Data: available upon request.
ISBN-10: 0-7922-6193-3
ISBN-13: 978-0-7922-6193-3

Printed in Spain

ABOUT THE AUTHOR

Jasper Becker has worked as a foreign correspondent for more than twenty years, fourteen of them based in Beijing, and has written four books on the region, including *Hungry Ghosts* (1996) and *The Chinese* (2000). Currently working for *The Independent* (London), he has also contributed features to NATIONAL GEOGRAPHIC magazine and many other periodicals, from the *International Herald Tribune* and the *Asian Wall Street Journal* to *The Spectator,* the *New Republic,* and *BusinessWeek.*

This book is set in Garamond 3, designed by Morris Fuller Benton and Thomas Maitland Cleland in the 1930s; Bank Gothic, designed at American Type Founders in 1930–33 by Morris Fuller Benton; and Futura, designed by Paul Renner in 1927.

Printed by Quebecor–Cayfosa, Barcelona, Spain, on 80-pound matte paper.

Dust jacket by Quebecor–Cayfosa, Barcelona, Spain. Color separation by Group 360 Visual Communications.

Three-piece case of black cloth spine #4000 by Brillianta. Side panels are red 80-pound text endsheet Prima 115 161 I by Geltex. Stamped in Kruz Luxor #420.